Creating Brand Strategy...
...for Your Life

Marva L. Goldsmith, AICI CIP

Branding
YOURSELF
AFTER
Age 50

www.marvagoldsmith.com

Branding
Yourself
After Age 50

Marva L. Goldsmith, AICI CIP

CONTRIBUTING EDITORS
Alicia M. Nails
Max Gordon

CONTRIBUTING AUTHORS
Art Lizza
Alford Day
Carla Dancy Smith
Satori Shakoor
Sue Thompson

First Publication: March 2009
Second Publication: September 2009

ISBN: 978-0-9765292-4-8

Acknowledgments

This book is dedicated to my mother. She is my hero. At the age of 51, after more than three decades spent working in the Detroit Police Department, my mother's determination and financial acumen enabled her to take the brave step of "early out."

She started working for the DPD right after high school at the age of 18, and continued working after marrying my father and giving birth to my sister (Marcia) and, two years later, me. After their divorce, she raised us, instilling in us the same determination and pride of accomplishment that led us to both become successful engineers in the 1980s—a time when female minorities were far from common.

Once Marcia and I were married, my mother opted for early retirement and moved to Tacoma, Washington, with her twin sister, who retired from Detroit Receiving Hospital. At the time of this writing, they are 76 years old. They have spent the past 25 years, a full third of their lives, living well without having to work another day in what has truly been their "Golden Age."

I began writing this book in the summer of 2008, while on my way to Little Rock, Arkansas, to attend my family reunion. Today my professional expertise is "image and branding," helping people to achieve their goals by presenting themselves and their companies in the best and most authentic way possible. With my December 5th birthday looming, the idea of turning 50 was often in my thoughts. Preparing for the inevitable reunion question of "What are you up to these days?" I pondered this looming milestone.

This book started as a reflection piece...therapy—*yes, self-imposed therapy*—and turned into something much more than I had imagined or planned. I am truly grateful to everyone who contributed to this book; including those whose stories you will read and others who were behind the scenes, editing, reading early drafts, or just cheering me on.

Special thanks go to Satori Shakoor, Lawrence Scott, Alford Day, Sue Thompson, Art Lizza, Christy Zorn, Carla Dancy, Alicia Nails, Max Gordon, Lisa Merriam, and Christa Davison for their contributions to the book. Thanks are also due to Walter O'Bryant, Vanessa Weathersby, Mary Artz, Frank Mitchell, and Lori DaGama for their review and comments.

I am especially grateful for my family and friends, who helped me usher in my second half-century of blissful living on a wintry evening in Detroit: Sheryl Shanklin, Preston Shanklin, Bernadine Miller, Andre DuPerry, Crystal Roberts, Michael Wagner, Tim and Rose Lucas, James Moore, Leland and Joyce Stein, George and Linda Stein, Vanessa Weathersby, Wesley Sewood, Sheila Spencer, Janna and Satchel Garrison, Alicia Nails, Venesta Jones, Tommy Stallworth, Nicole Wells, and especially my loving sister, Marcia Jackson, who made my celebration possible.

I'd like to extend my gratitude, too, to the pioneers of personal branding: Tom Peters, credited with coining the phrase and starting the revolution, and Peter Montoya, whose book *The Brand Called You* led me to the exploration of self as a product.

I hope this book will inspire some direction or purpose, or simply encourage you to live out your bliss...and to be your own "best brand."

Happy 50th!

Contents

INTRODUCTION

A Flight of Fancy at 50

July 24, 2008

I hear and feel the familiar thud of the plane's doors closing tightly, then the plane shudders into motion. We roll toward the runway, and I begin to say a little prayer as we prepare for takeoff. Halfway through the prayer, it hits me! I open one eye in excitement, but then decide to finish the prayer—always a good idea before takeoff—before returning to my inspiration.

Finally, after months of agonizing thought, I know what I want to do for my birthday. It's not just any birthday. On December 5th, I will turn 50.

The pressure to do something in celebration of that all-important 50th birthday is enormous. Well, at least it has been for me. Think about it: The half-century mark!

"How old are you?" I imagine being asked.

"Half a century," I will say.

Shall I have a party? Should I have it in Detroit, where I've lived most of my life...or in Maryland, where I currently reside? Decisions, decisions. The pressure!

Perhaps I'll just take the "no worries" solution and live vicariously through my sister—retroactively. She

1

had a fabulous 50th celebration two years earlier. Her last guest didn't leave until 4 o'clock the next morning. I had a blast! We danced, laughed, drank, ate, then we danced some more. As a matter of fact, I seem to have many friends and family members turning 50 these days. Perhaps instead of hosting one big party, I will celebrate my birthday at every other 50th celebration I attend.

I thought about going to a mind and body cleansing retreat—some type of health farm, rejuvenation spa, or women's retreat. I researched Sedona, the Crossings in Austin, and Life Launch in Santa Barbara, where I could indulge in healthy exercise and food, as well as yoga, meditation, daily massage, sitar music, bean sprouts—you know, the whole transcendental experience. Rise with the sun and reflect on life. Just take a "time out." Leave the Black*(crack)*berry and the laptop at home and take time to just BE. I'm still thinking about this idea—it sounds pretty refreshing.

I also thought about taking a cruise in the Caribbean with someone special. Or, going island hopping with a group of friends, for fun, shopping, cosmos, and just mixing it up—somewhat the opposite end of the spectrum from the "cleansing retreat" idea. I haven't ruled out those options.

Since it will take me another five months to write this book, you may find out that I did the spa trip or took a cruise after all. (In fact, I know I would enjoy finishing up the final writing of this book on a beach in St. Lucia, Puerto Rico, or St. Martin?)

But what was it, you may be wondering, that "hit me" as my flight was taking off?

You're holding it right now.

I thought, *I'll write a book on turning 50!*

An old idea with a new direction

Okay, it's not a new idea. Many people have written books about turning 50. Many of the books are celebrity autobiographies—the personal lives and careers, up to and including the 50-year milestone, of the famous and infamous.

This book will be different. This book isn't by or for people who think that their best years lay behind them, for those who long for the glory and smooth skin of their salad days. No, *this* book will focus on the rest of us and will be a guide to branding yourself *after* age 50. It will *not* be about nostalgia or the search for the Fountain of Youth but about the rest—and the best—that is yet to come. New beginnings. Renewal. Reinvention.

What is personal branding?

What is personal branding—and why do you need to think about it? According to Peter Montoya, a personal brand is "an identity that stimulates precise, meaningful perceptions in its audience about the values and qualities the person stands for." These perceptions vary as you move from one "domain" to another: home, business, community, and/or school. Your brand in your "business" domain is not going to be the same as your brand in your "home" domain: that is, your kids, significant other or parents will not describe you using the same words as your business colleagues.

Personal branding is all about differentiating yourself from the rest of the "market" out there. To do that, you need to know what about *you* is unique and compelling. Ultimately, branding involves three important components, the three Ps: personality, position, and promise.

- **PERSONALITY**—A successful brand is packaged in such a way that you distinguish yourself from others, while supporting the vision that you have for your future. This does not mean you have to dress or behave in some outré fashion, only that **YOU** need to highlight your best features to be easily recognizable. Your packaging is an advertisement of the product. So, be careful to send the right message at all times.

- **POSITION**— A successful brand provides added to value in order to determine its relative position amongst other products. The most successful brands can be described in a single sentence or phrase. "Like a rock" suggests that Chevy trucks are tough. "We'll leave the light on for you" says you're always welcome at Motel 6. What about **YOU**? Maybe "Pat Smith always gets things done," or "Terry Jones knows everything about sailing." If you are incredibly successful, sometimes your brand can be described by a single word, as were Kleenex and Xerox. Think: Oprah, Madonna, Gandhi.

- **PROMISE**—A successful brand promises a particular experience. Online auctioneer eBay says "Buy it. Sell it. Love it." The whole experience is suggested by these six words: customers will find it easy to buy and sell, and they will be pleased with the results. What promise do **YOU** offer? Maybe you're a top-notch CPA who offers "worry-free tax preparation" or a coach for runners who wants to "train without pain."

Read the following excerpt from *The 22 Immutable Laws of Branding* (2002), by Al Ries and Laura Ries. I've substituted the word "**YOU**" where it applies:

4

"…[B]randing in the marketplace is very similar to branding on the ranch. A branding program should be designed to differentiate YOU from all the 'cattle on the range.' Even if all the other cattle on the range look pretty much alike…the objective is to create in the mind of the prospect the perception that there is no other product on the market quite like YOU."

For more on branding, see Chapter 5

A new direction

I started my branding and personal development company, Marva Goldsmith & Associates (MG&A), in September 2001. I left my job at a utility company, thinking that starting the company was just something I would do while waiting for a C-level position (or at least a VP spot) to materialize. I had read an article that stated for every $100,000 in salary you seek, you needed to allow 12 to 18 months for your job search. So, I started MG&A as a placeholder, something to list on my resume as an "in the meantime" activity.

After a few months of self-employment, my fear of ending up as a bag lady was all but gone, surpassed by the joy I felt while helping others reshape their personal and professional images. Soon I stopped looking for that C-level job altogether and started reinventing the brand known as Marva Goldsmith. This book offers a glimpse into the process I used to reinvent myself (*before* age 50) as well as an idea of how you can apply it to your own lives—at any age.

Supporting characters

Since at the time I began this writing I was not yet 50, I could not legitimately offer the full experience of branding myself after age 50, so I invited a few other people to contribute to this book.

- **Art Lizza** is the primary case study we'll follow. "Downsized" *after* age 50, Art found his passion as a writer and is now working to reinvent himself as a full-time author.

- **Sue Thompson** started a motivation and public speaking business and lost 75 pounds—and she did it all *after* turning 50.

- **Larry Scott** left his comfortable corporate position in sales at age 48 to start his own air conditioning business. He's now working to build his entrepreneurial brand after age 50.

- **Satori Shakoor** celebrated her 50th birthday in fine form—by successfully competing in a bodybuilding competition.

- **Carla Dancy Smith** began her master's degree program at American University at the age of 50.

- **Alford Day** is a businessman in healthcare who, after a very bad day at his multimillion-dollar company, found himself having to begin all over again—after age 50.

If you're wondering how to kick it into gear *after* the **Big 5-0**, you'll get plenty of inspiration and information from this book. Even if your reinvention strategy doesn't include starting a company or going back to school, you are already a consultant with a brand of your own. If you are over 50, or approaching the "Golden Age," you have been developing a set of transferable skills for years. Most likely these skills are still needed somewhere— even if it's not with your current or former employer, or even in the business world.

Over the past seven years, I have completely rewritten my professional script and roles: I've transitioned from being an engineer, federal lobbyist, and mid-level utility executive to being an image consultant, brand coach, national speaker, trainer, and entrepreneur. My resume is *not* defined by my past experience in corporate America.

Instead, it focuses on my desire for the next 15 years: to be a nationally recognized, highly sought-after, *well-paid* speaker and consultant who creates experiences that transform corporations, organizations, and, most importantly, individuals.

This book has been written using my experiences with transformation. Many of you reading this book will find yourself asking the same questions I asked myself in the face of change and surprises, especially the big question: *Is this a crisis...or an opportunity in disguise?* It all depends on your perspective. Here, the focus will be on you, and your brand. What should you do now that the employment game has changed? If you fully engage, complete the exercises in this book, and *get into action*, a year from now you may look back and say, **job uncertainty was the best thing that ever happened to me.**

To make this happen, this book will help you address three questions:

1. *What do I want?*

2. *How do I get from "then" to "now"?*

3. *If not now, when?*

Present...tense?

First, let's assess the present. Even at the age of 50, some of us have not fully explored the first question. Perhaps you've never taken the time to *ask* the question at all. It's easy to get caught up in everyday living, unconscious living—cruise control. I don't know about you, but I feel as if I just looked up one day and there it was—I was almost 50. It snuck up almost without warning. It's easy to understand how busy lives can detract from our ability to take time out and answer this important question of what we *really* want.

Throughout this book, you will find stories written by those who are living in their own "Golden Age," people who know just what they want and are currently in hot pursuit of it. You will also read the stories of individuals who face branding challenges that relate to turning 50. You know, the people who find themselves at the half-century mark and suddenly wondering what they want to be when they grow up.

Although the focus of this book is on your professional life, it can also change your personal life, as this book can be used as a vehicle to explore the pathways of your hopes and dreams to discover your **life's purpose**.

The "Golden Age" begins at 50

Before we proceed, let me define the term "Golden Age." For some, the term will conjure up images of the sitcom, the *Golden Girls* television show—that is, cute and funny, but *old*.

GOLD is such a precious metal. It's been used almost since the dawn of human history to display wealth and importance, and it has inherent qualities as well. Being relatively soft and malleable, it is an efficient conductor of both heat and electricity. Gold is resistant to the effects of moisture, oxygen, and corrosive elements.

People who have lived to their 50th year are like gold. We have certainly encountered a few corrosive elements, have had to be malleable and flexible, and have experienced many electric moments. We are precious metals. Indeed, at the Golden Age, we *should be* "highly sought-after" precious metals.

On the following pages, we'll explore the **Golden Age** together. What's in store for us? How can we best approach this wonderful time in our lives? What do we want? How are we *being* at 50?

As I reflect on this "turning 50" project, I hope this book has a broader reach, a wider appeal, and a more profound impact than a 50th birthday celebration. I hope it exhilarates others as much as any party, a spa retreat, or even a lavish trip to an exotic destination, and brings a spark of renewal and rejuvenation to me *and* to you.

Consider this book to be an invitation to my birthday celebration. My birthday wish for you is that you will **commit to transformation** and you will begin the work of branding yourself after age 50. Some of you will find your transformation to be a reinvention. That's a positive form of change. Don't waste a moment!

The time to begin is **now**!

Carpe Diem!

CHAPTER 1

What's Age Got To Do With It?

As of this writing I am single…and looking. Hello?!

I went on a date a few months ago with a man I met over a popular Internet dating site. My date worked in the entertainment industry. After a couple of hours, we exchanged Internet dating horror stories—now that's always fun to do! We talked about how, during your first face-to-face meeting, it quickly becomes obvious (sometimes painfully so) if your date has a much exaggerated sense of self, has used someone else's pictures, has led a really hard life since registering with the site, or is a master at reinventing the truth.

My eyes became as big as saucers when my date confessed that he did not tell the truth about two items in his online dating profile. *Please don't tell me you're married!* I can't remember the first trivial fib he confessed to, but the second was about his age. He had listed himself as 48 years old, when in fact he had just turned 50. He explained that entertainment is a very competitive industry, and he was sensitive to the stigma of being an "old man" in a "young person's" industry where people are routinely shuffled in and out of jobs based on others' perceptions that veterans may not be "fresh." I was reminded of a lyric from Harry Chapin's hit WOLD:

11

"They said they wanted the 'young sound,' when they let me go."

For some, the idea of turning 50 is daunting. For others, it's a new adventure. But, clearly my date had an issue with perception. Later I considered his situation, and decided that he needed to ask himself some tough questions. How could he manage the way others perceive him? How could he prepare himself for what he believes to be the inevitable and untimely demise of his career? How could he effectively brand himself as a valuable, contributing player in a youth-focused industry, even after the age of 50?

Turning 50 is different than turning 30 or 40

When I turned 30, I felt like a grownup, as though I had suddenly blossomed into adulthood. Thirty had a very mature ring to it. For most people, your 30s are the time you become the principal star of your own mini-series: your career is progressing and you have (consciously or not) established your personal "brand" in your work and community lives. People expect a certain level and range of experience from you based on what they know that you usually deliver.

You are making money. You are making significant life choices during this decade. Professionally and personally, the opportunities before you seem limitless. Most significantly, you feel as though you have plenty of time left to choose among them.

Your sense of immortality begins to fade somewhat by your 40s, and you aggressively pursue professional and personal goals. For many, that means nurturing and raising little people, too. At 40, you are in the headlong rush of real life. You are in the big leagues, playing the grownup game with skill and purpose, with a great deal of self-assurance and confidence. After all, you have accumulated a fair amount of experience. Your decisions affect others tremendously, both at home and at work, so you direct your focus on choosing wisely and making sound decisions. You are still young enough to play, but old enough to take full responsibility for your actions. Perhaps most important of all: You are responsible and accountable.

I think of turning 40 with glee—yes, absolute glee. I was a triple threat! My body, brain, and bank account were simultaneously in full throttle. In retrospect, I was fearless. *What the heck?* I thought. I was divorced, didn't have any children—what better time would there be to make some changes—take some risks? I made a bold, life-altering decision to go back to school full-time, took a year off from the corporate world, and went to Harvard. Fun! Exciting! Geez, me, at Harvard! I met people from all over the world. I had given myself a gift that significantly changed the trajectory of my life.

Nobody warned me about turning 50

Whenever I hear those first strains of George Clinton and Funkadelic's classic *Flashlight*, I still jump up to dance. I still make silly jokes with my sister that only we understand. I still eat peanut butter right out of the jar. How can I possibly be turning 50?

I read in *O Magazine* (Oprah approved it, so it must be true) that every day 6,000 American women turn 50 years old. So, I know there is a huge "amen corner" backing up my claim, that turning 50 feels different from any other decade changeover. Physically, and perhaps emotionally, something is clearly different about 50. First, there's my physical inventory. I am certainly entering my 50s with a different physicality. Some of the physical changes are inevitable and apparently permanent. It appears that the laws of elasticity and gravity have serious implications for skin, tendons, and muscles as well. You can only stretch or stitch some of these body parts so far before they refuse to spring back or stay put.

I have accepted my own physical changes, like weight gain and hair loss. I have begun to do what I can to slow my body's natural aging process, eating "goo-gobs"' of antioxidants, and joining both Weight Watchers and Curves. In fact, I've been told that I don't look 50 at all. (Thank you, Mom, for good genes.)

Inevitably, there is the post-50 professional inventory, and some comparisons between what we had hoped to achieve and what we have actually accomplished or become. Some of our career choices may seem permanent. But must they be? Some opportunities may have passed us by...but have they really been "lost" to us?

What about new opportunities and choices? Are they still limitless? Is it still possible to be a fearless and confident star going into our sixth decade?

I have used terms like star and fearless and confidence to describe the onset of my 30s and 40s, but my focus here will be what will mark this decade of the 50s—for me and for you. For those years we need a new set of words: words like courageous, relentless, strong, happy, peaceful, graceful, exuberant, wise, spiritual, intuitive, and blessed come to mind.

> **EXERCISE:**
>
> *The mind never stops working. It is important to have a place to record your thoughts as you read. I rarely read a book without a pen in my hand. As you go through this book, certain stories, ideas, and questions will resonate with you. Get in the habit of writing those precious thoughts down—for an example, answer the following question:*
>
> *What are you thinking? (Don't say, 'Nothing.' That's absolutely impossible.)*

_____

_____

_____

_____

_____

_____

_____

_____

_____

_____

_____

CHAPTER 2

Problem... or Opportunity?

A classic parable

I do not recall when or from whom I first heard this, or when, but the message is one for the ages.

A farmer's donkey fell into an abandoned well. The donkey cried for hours while the farmer pondered what to do. Finally, he decided that since the donkey had lived a long life, and the well had to be filled in anyway, he would simply say a few words and bury the donkey in the well. He asked his neighbors to help him, and everyone began shoveling dirt into the well. At first, the donkey cried even louder. Then, to everyone's amazement, he became quiet. Curious, the farmer looked into the well and was astonished to see that with each shovel of dirt that hit his back, the donkey would simply shake it off and step up onto it. It was not long before the donkey was able to step over the edge of the well and trot happily away.

MORAL: Shake it off and step up!

Uncertain times, surprising opportunities

Crisis…depression…recession…or even just plain hard times…whatever you call the current international financial situation, the impact is the same: we are faced with a very uncertain employment and economic future.

Every decade brings some form of economic turmoil. In the 1970s, the U.S. economy saw high energy prices, high inflation, and high interest rates. The front-page headlines grew shrill with warnings of yet more layoffs and company closings. (Sound familiar?) During the 80s and 90s, the words restructuring and downsizing became staples in our business vocabulary. And now, a decade into the 21st century, we are seeing numerous industries shutting down, jobs moving overseas, and a demand for new skills. Even the "Big 3" U.S. automakers and "Big Blue" are no longer big. Marvin Gaye sang, "There are only three things for sure—taxes, death, and trouble."

I would modify the list to include *change*.

Change is an unstoppable force. Benjamin Disraeli, a 19th-century British writer and statesman, said, "Change is inevitable. Change is constant." For example, even in the best of times, you could still lose your job or source of income. It doesn't matter whether you lose your job in a mass layoff, during a time of economic turmoil, or when everything is booming for everyone else. The moment you lose your job, you are at a crossroad.

John F. Kennedy once observed, "When written in Chinese, the word 'crisis' is composed of two characters. One represents danger, and the other represents opportunity." So the question you must ask yourself is, "Will I treat this circumstance as a crisis or as an opportunity?"

I have learned to create "opportunity" from almost any set of circumstances—whether self-imposed or unplanned. After 20 years, I chose to leave my comfortable corporate position at a major utility company and pursue my dreams. Seven years later, I found myself surrounded by comrades in their 50s who were in the midst of "un-planned career outages."

Many people who face unemployment for the first time after 20 or 25 years of continuous employment are justifiably frightened after having been busily engaged in their careers. Some are high-flyers who have done nothing wrong—indeed, some were the driving forces behind the success of their respective companies, yet nevertheless found themselves in the position of having to begin over again.

Remember the parable? Deep in a well, the donkey who was facing a crisis hesitated at first, but soon recognized it as an opportunity. Here's the deal: nothing is going to change the fact that you've lost your job, or promotion, or the funds you've invested. You cannot wish that job, promotion, pension, or golden parachute back into existence. Once the genie is out of the bottle, it's not going back inside. So now what? You need to learn to recognize what's being shoveled onto your head as the key to stepping up and out.

EXERCISE

It is the time to take inventory. What can you do in the meantime? Is it possible there is a bright side— an opportunity—masquerading as doom and gloom? Is it possible to launch a new career, land a new job, or start a new business, even in this economy?

_____

_____

_____

_____

_____

_____

_____

_____

_____

_____

_____

_____

_____

_____

The Iceberg exercise

When I first encountered this exercise, I was a student in Georgetown University's Leadership Coaching program. The model was developed by Alexander Caillet (© 2002 Gunn Partners). The premise is that your thoughts affect your feelings; your feelings influence your behaviors; your behaviors manifest as results. At the core of the chain of progression are your beliefs.

The iceberg metaphor works well. Results and behaviors are what we experience or see. Underneath the surface, and the most potentially powerful, are what we cannot see—thoughts, feelings and beliefs.

EXAMPLE

Current State: You're looking for a job, and your resume has done a great job of securing interviews. Yet so far you have not landed a position. Why not? Let's examine the situation in an "iceberg" view.

THE "TIP" OF THE ICEBERG
- **Results**: Unsuccessful interviews

- **Behaviors:** Project an air of desperation and lack of self-confidence. Lackluster answers and performance, including unclear goals, no value proposition (cannot articulate the value provided to the company).

BENEATH THE SURFACE
- **Feelings:** Depressed. Scared. Resigned.

- **Thoughts:** What's the point? They'll probably give the job to some 30-year-old kid anyway.

- **Beliefs:** It's too late for me to get a new job. It's less expensive for companies to hire younger people. I'm too old to start something new.

What if you could change the **beliefs** that underlie every-thing else? What if, like the donkey in the well, you could view the idea of change as an opportunity instead of a crisis, and anticipated success rather than defeat?

- Imagine these **beliefs**: "My experiences are valuable. I have unique skills that create additional value."

- Those beliefs might lead to these **thoughts**: "I have a lot to offer this company, but if nothing else, I will make some valuable contacts."

- Those thoughts might engender these **feelings**: optimism, self-confidence, excitement.

- These can lead to more positive **behaviors:** fluid responses, an air of confidence and competence, engaging conversation, attentive body language, a firm handshake, and a reassuring smile.

- And great **results**: a successful interview!

EXERCISE

First, identify what's going on in your professional life now, and what upcoming or recent changes might affect you. (For example, you may have learned that your boss is accepting a job with another company, that your company is offering early retirement packages—or, that your pink slip has just arrived.) Then describe your desired state.

Describe your current state (RESULTS)

_____

_____

_____

_____

What BEHAVIORS have you exhibited that support these results?

_____

_____

_____

_____

How are you FEELING about these results?

_____

_____

_____

_____

Describe your THOUGHTS:

_____

_____

_____

_____

What BELIEFS are central to (or at the core of) these thoughts?

_____

_____

_____

_____

Now describe your desired RESULTS:

_____

_____

_____

_____

_____

_____

_____

25

What BEHAVIORS support these results?

_____

_____

_____

_____

_____

_____

_____

How would you FEEL about these results?

_____

_____

_____

_____

_____

_____

_____

Describe your THOUGHTS right now:

_____

_____

_____

_____

_____

_____

_____

What BELIEFS are at the core of the thoughts?

_____

_____

_____

_____

_____

_____

_____

CHAPTER 3

The Pursuit of Happiness

When I really thought about my pursuit, it wasn't about the career, or a new business; it was about personal freedom. **I live to be free!**

Ten years ago, I had begun to feel gray, dull, colorless—like the skies that paint the Detroit winter mornings. My life had taken unexpected turns. My career, though meaningful, was not fulfilling. I felt a need for retooling and reinvention. So, I took a leap of faith and went to graduate school.

In plotting your course, the first question you'll need to answer is simply, "What do you want?"

Before you assess where you want to go, it is helpful to take inventory of where you have been. Every moment we've already lived is in the past; so we will call it **"Then."** To begin your journey, you will capture (in Chapter 4) your own personal "Then."

You are on a journey from "Then" to "Now!"

My Own "Then"

Let's confine "Then" to the events and developments of just the preceding decade. As an example, here's what my "Then" inventory would look like:

29

My 40s began this way:

- Great career, but bored and questioning what would be coming next

- Single, without children

- Tired of the harsh winters in Detroit

My 40s ended this way:

- Harvard graduate, entrepreneur, image consultant who literally gets paid to shop, trainer with clients located from coast to coast, member of the Board of the Association of Image Consultants International (AICI.org), author and public speaker.

- Still single, but happily looking; still without children, but having affected the lives of hundreds (hopefully thousands by the time you read this) of at-risk and incarcerated youth through my workbooks and workshops.

- Escaped the harsh winters of Detroit to a softer, gentler east coast way of living

- Physically a bit wider and with more gray hairs—but definitely a whole lot wiser!

This is a quick summary to give you the idea of what to record. (I have learned to hit the highlights.) You may want to spend more time on your "Then" story. Let's use Art as an example of what you may want to record...

Art's Story

Then: Corporate Success in the Decade of My 40s

My wife and I were living in our dream house—an 1847 country farmhouse that needed some work and TLC. Thankfully, we still live there today. When I turned 40, our daughter was 8 years old and an honor student.

When I joined my firm in 1978, it was a collection of free-thinking individuals working out of the basement of the owner/publisher's home. By 1992, as I entered my 40s, the company published scholarly texts.

I was the boss's right-hand man, overseeing all publishing production operations. I had a good share of executive responsibilities, and a large share of IT and telecommunications functions. I had a production staff of 16 and general authority over the entire company.

We were a growing company, bursting at the seams—running out of both office and warehouse space, at multiple locations.

In 1993 we found a stop-gap solution to our growing pains. I was moved to a building with sufficient warehouse space and just enough office space for the production department. Though just seven miles from the main office, this satellite facility might as well have been light-years away.

Interpersonal communication began to suffer almost immediately after the move. Before, editorial staff could simply walk down the hall to my office to ask a question. Now, they didn't consult, not even by phone. They began making unilateral decisions that would later have detrimental consequences for our publishing program.

The biggest blow, however, came not from corporate operations, but from Mother Nature. On Friday, July 8, 1994, massive thunderstorms hammered northeastern New Jersey. Our new satellite office was overrun with floodwaters that submerged the parking lot and destroyed seven of our employees' cars. Some of my staff escaped ahead of the flood, and a brave few individuals attempted to wade out and were later rescued by volunteers manning rowboats. In the end, I managed to get the remaining eight or nine staff members outside safely and loaded into the back of a tractor trailer, the only vehicle able to make it through the cresting waters as the storm subsided. Like a good captain, I stayed, determined to go down with the ship.

We had expanded to the satellite offices only a year before, yet in addition to the problems caused by the flood it was apparent that we were running out of space, again. The good news, at least, was that executive management realized that the dual-office arrangement was unacceptable.

I had no trouble convincing my boss to put me in charge of finding and securing new quarters, sufficient to reunite the company—and to move us literally to higher ground!

On July 3, 1995—just a few days shy of the anniversary of the big flood—the production department moved again, this time into our brand new digs in Mahwah. We were soon joined by the rest of the company's staff, the week following the July 4th holiday.

Our momentous business growth continued. That month we acquired publishing rights to the education list of a major New York publisher. We next purchased a smaller publishing house and several other additions. We were growing faster than ever before...maybe too fast. Despite our successes, storm clouds had begun to gather. We were always pushing, always trying to accomplish more, and always focusing on growth. This led to some serious job stress.

A few years later, as the millennium approached, a crisis erupted with a key employee, one I had promoted to a top management post during the satellite office days. There were some very serious abuses of power, and more critically and hurtfully, abuses of people.

I had been so involved in general business operations, as well as orchestrating the move to Mahwah, that I simply did not see the problems developing. I also had a serious blind spot with respect to this individual. HR learned of the new manager's abuses through exit interviews with other valuable and talented staff members who had become so disgusted that they chose to quit. Consequently, my boss learned about the abuses, became infuriated, and ultimately forced me to act. The incident caused a rift between me and the manager—a rift that would never fully heal. This was the worst leadership failure in my career.

Around that same time, in 1998, my daughter—my only child—left for college. The empty nest syndrome hit me harder than I could ever have imagined. My wife, now suddenly and almost completely free from the day-to-day responsibilities of parenting, seized the opportunity to ramp up her photography business. I decided to tackle the house restoration projects still to be done. But, there I was, surrounded by my saws, hammers and power tools, and wondering, "Why the hell am I doing this?" That's when I realized that I felt very much alone in the world.

I became depressed. I began abusing alcohol, which made my depression worse. I came to fear everything. Most of all, despite the fact that at no time in life did I have more "stuff," I developed a chronic and ever-deepening fear of losing everything!

Turning 50: Art's Pinnacle...and His Plunge

I have never seen much point in celebrating my birthday, even the so-called milestone ones. When I walked into my office in 2002 on my 50th birthday, I found 50 boxes of my favorite treat. That was pretty strong evidence that my production staff did not share my view on birthdays. Mallomars® were stacked everywhere—on my desk, on

33

the shelves, windowsills—everywhere. It was an auspicious beginning to my 50s. The Mallomars® were evidence that "my people" both respected and, for the most part, liked me. I always tried to be a compassionate manager and mentor, and to protect my staff when they made honest mistakes. They seemed to have forgiven my major error in judgment about the abusive manager, and for the previous seven years I had retained all of my book production editors. In many respects, these were the pinnacle years of my publishing career. I had a great staff and the respect of my peers. My daughter graduated from college and came home again. Things should have been getting better, but unfortunately, I still had persistent, underlying personal problems.

In late spring of 2003, my boss called me into his office. He swore me to confidence, confessing his decision to sell the company. At first I did not believe him; he had talked about selling before. But, when he told me this time, I was convinced that he meant it. He said he had lost the drive and lost the "fire in his belly" for this business. This was a highly competitive man who, if he could not do something well enough to compete, he would not do it at all. I knew he was done.

He also asked me to resign from the company. It was largely my own fault. While I had made some progress taming my personal demons, even in the midst of professional success, my depressive moods and my sometimes erratic performance were burdens he could no longer afford—not as he focused on selling the company. I tendered my resignation on July 31.

In the days leading up to my departure, I tried to stay positive. I even fantasized walking out of the office on that last Friday afternoon and feeling the "lifting" of that great and proverbial "weight from my shoulders" that we so often hear about. But my real experience was nothing of the sort.

Instead, on that next Monday, at the age of 53, I was unemployed for the first time in my life. Despite my very generous 18-month severance package, I was in a state of utter panic, consumed with an irrational need to find a new job *immediately*. I set out on a frantic but fruitless job search that lasted nearly three years.

Then one day I changed my mind. I decided, "Let's change course."

And I wasn't alone. The company sold a year and a half later for $71 million, putting most of the 100 remaining employees out of work.

Turning 50: Art's "Road Not Taken"

> *"When you come to a fork in the road, take it!"*
> —Yogi Berra

In my final days with the company, I had thought about trying to land a production director position with a small university press. My thinking was this: something non-profit, university subsidized, with a little less stress, a lot less emphasis on making profit, and a smaller, more manageable workload. I saw myself wearing one of those corduroy sport jackets with the patches on the elbows, walking around a quaint university town in Hush Puppies, looking like a psychology professor. Maybe I'd even take up pipe smoking to complete the look. My impression was that university press positions were highly prized and immensely fulfilling—after all, they published important stuff, even if some of it was rather obscure. Well... that was then.

Recently, one of these "ideal" positions actually came open. I pounced. I soon received a call from the director of the press to schedule a conference call interview with the search committee. "I believe I'm the first candidate he's called," I told myself. "I believe I am in."

In the days leading up to the interview, with three years of perspective since having left my life in the corporate world, I began to have second thoughts—serious second thoughts. Did I really want to go back to what I had done for nearly 30 years? Did I really want to go back to doing something I could probably do in my sleep? What would happen if they actually offered me this job? Was it *truly* what I wanted now? I realized that something deep within me had really, almost pervasively, changed.

Subconsciously, these thoughts must have weighed heavily on me; I blew the interview big time. I was simply not myself. I was nervous, I vacillated, I rambled. To my horror, we somehow got off on a discussion of my worst leadership failure—*at length*. I still have no idea exactly how that happened, but I remember feeling powerless to regain control of the conversation.

Bye-bye elbow patches

So, what exactly changed during those three years? First, I gained control over my problem with alcohol. Without that, no progress would have been possible.

Second, I survived three years of unemployment—long enough to know that there is indeed life after corporate. I am still here, still living in my now (nearly!) refurbished farmhouse, still married to a woman who adores me, and the proud father of my daughter, who's now a 28-year-old woman.

Third, I lost my fear. At 56, my journey has led me to control. I now control fear; fear does not control me. The most joyful part is that I have recaptured the very confidence that enabled me to join a start-up company way back when I began this journey.

I realized that what I wanted was a challenge. And something else—I realized that there was something I have wanted to do since I was 12, something I repressed for 40 years: **I want to write.** That is my answer to the first question addressed in this book. "What do you want?" **I want to write.** I also know that to get from "Then" to "Now" will take hard work.

Art: confident, prepared for the challenge, resilient, skilled, creative, and loved.

Coach's Check-In

Did anything in Art's story resonate with you? Could this have been a chapter in your book? Do you know others with the same story? It is interesting to note that when Art went to the interview for what he thought was his "dream job," his heart was not in it.

At this point in our lives, we are looking for work that makes our hearts sing. If we have the luxury of discovery, we will find or create an opportunity in which the heart sings and our bills are paid. This is indeed the ultimate opportunity.

EXERCISE

Take this time to begin creating that opportunity for yourself. Capture in writing the thoughts that Art's story stirred up for you. You'll need them as we go along!

_____

_____

_____

_____

_____

_____

_____

_____

_____

_____

_____

_____

_____

_____

_____

_____

Create the change you want to see: Using the SWOT analysis as a personal inventory

Harland David "Colonel" Sanders began building his Kentucky Fried Chicken empire at the age of 65.

It is never too late to start a second career—to move from "Then" to "Now." So, just how does Art go about branding himself as a writer, at the age of 56?

Art acknowledged that the main requirement would be hard work. He's right. So, let's get started. The first step is to conduct a SWOT analysis of the product, which in this case is **Art**. SWOT is an acronym for Strengths, Weaknesses, Opportunities, and Threats. You can use the SWOT analysis to help identify and document your personal pluses and minuses:

SWOT

INTERNAL

STRENGTHS

WEAKNESSES

EXTERNAL

OPPORTUNITIES

THREATS

Art's SWOT

Strengths
- Excellent command of the English language, with a strong vocabulary and writing skills

- Maturity and experience from 30 years in scholarly publishing, yet fresh and up-to-date

- Ability to remain impartial, to see the merit and the folly of all sides of an issue or a story

- Adept at constructing and presenting strong, logical, and persuasive arguments from multiple perspectives; capable of recognizing, respecting, and understanding opposing viewpoints

Weaknesses
- Self doubt about being able to make a living, particularly in the short term, so that I can segue from my temporary retail job without "losing the farm." I imagine a crystallizing moment when I can calmly, and with immense satisfaction, tender my resignation to the department store because my income from writing has surpassed that from retail, and I can focus all of my attention and energies in that direction.

- Another aspect of self-doubt—the knowledge that it will be very hard work to build a gainful writing career while having to work full time at a mind numbing, spirit-sapping occupation— scares the hell out of me.

Opportunities
- Limitless—registered on one freelance Internet site that seems to post 20–30 new opportunities every day, and that's only one site; have current *Writer's Marketplace* with listings of over 3,500 publishers or places to publish

- Range—the beauty of writing is that it can be applied to anything from advertising to business to culture to art to history to current affairs

Threats
- Personal energy—Will be draining to get my writing career off the ground while I'm tethered to a full-time job for the health insurance and income it provides. I feel fairly positive about this, as the combination of fervent desire and financial necessity make for a powerful dual force to make it happen.

COACH'S CHECK-IN

Let's stop here so that you can catch up. I did tell you that this is a workbook, right?

You have read Art's story and reviewed his SWOT analysis. Chapter 4 is all about you!

To begin plotting your path, capture in writing your own personal "Then" inventory in the next chapter.

CHAPTER 4

So, What Do <u>You</u> Want?

Establishing your brand identity

Your first step on the journey of branding yourself after age 50 is to begin writing your "Then" statement. Ask yourself all sorts of open-ended questions like these:

- How do you see yourself and your accomplishments over the past ten years?

- What would you say were the defining moments in your life during that time?

- What major decisions have you (or others) made that affected you?

- What led you to the path you have been on?

- Is it your joy in life to walk this path, or is this road one that is paved by necessity or responsibility?

- What are your major accomplishments, or your life challenges?

- What changes occurred over the last decade?

Answering these questions will help to define "Then" for you just as Art and I did in Chapter 3.

43

EXERCISE
Define your "Then" by asking yourself open-ended questions. Use extra paper or create a journal so that you can revisit and add on to each exercise.

Are you warmed up yet?

I described Art's attributes as confident, prepared for challenge, resilient, skilled, creative, and loved. What specific attributes can you use to describe yourself?

_____

_____

_____

_____

_____

Art described his goal succinctly: **"I want to write."** What are your goals for this branding exercise? What do you hope to accomplish?

List up to three goals. The more succinctly you can list your goals, the easier it will be to work towards them.

_____

_____

_____

_____

_____

Your SWOT

With your goal(s) in mind, complete your own SWOT analysis using the spaces provided on the following pages, on a separate sheet of paper, or in a journal or notebook. (You have my permission to make copies of these SWOT exercises.)

Your internal **Strengths** include your inherent abilities, your skills, your qualifications and credentials—all the things that you can control that can help you attain your goals.

Your internal **Weaknesses** are the things that control you, things that will hold you back from attaining your goals unless you address them head on. Your weaknesses may include a lack of certain skills or abilities, a disposition that is inherently negative (glass half-empty mentality), or the need for certain credentials.

Opportunities and **Threats** are external forces that can either help or hinder you from reaching your goals. Think globally, especially as you describe your opportunities and threats. Are there opportunities presented by technology or the Internet that can help you reach your goals? How are you capitalizing on the explosion of social networking opportunities such as Facebook, Twitter, LinkedIn, and a galaxy of other tools that are literally at your fingertips? What networking vehicles or blogs are available within your industry? And don't try to tell me that that stuff is "just for kids," because you'd be surprised how many grandparents rely on the Internet today to keep in touch with their far-flung families. If you ignore the fact that this is how many people communicate these days, you're missing the boat. Get on board and get online!

Think past your immediate base of friends and family; who is in your network that can assist you? More importantly, think about how they might be of help. Do you know others who have achieved goals similar to yours?

Who else is doing what you want to do—and doing it well? What gates did they open? What did they have to overcome to reach this goal?

Self-assessment is never easy. Ask friends, relatives and co-workers to help you identify your strengths and weaknesses. Consider copying the following pages and asking others to give you an honest appraisal. You might be surprised at what other people think your strengths and weaknesses are.

This is also a good time to take a few online assessments (Strengths Finder, Myers-Briggs, Keirsey Temperament, etc.). These assessments may also help you articulate your strengths and weaknesses.

Your SWOT

Strengths

_____

_____

_____

_____

_____

_____

_____

_____

Weaknesses

_____

_____

_____

_____

_____

_____

_____

_____

Opportunities

_____

_____

_____

_____

_____

_____

_____

_____

Threats

_____

_____

_____

_____

_____

_____

_____

_____

Unique selling proposition: Your sweet spot

The information you gather and document by doing the SWOT exercise can help you formulate what is called your *unique selling proposition* (USP). Essentially this is exactly what it sounds like: your USP is what you can offer that no one else can or does.

In *Reality in Advertising*, Reeves (1961) defined the three parts that make up a unique selling proposition. We'll focus on the first segment to help define USP for personal branding:

1. Each advertisement must make a proposition to the consumer. Not just words, not just product puffery, not just show-window advertising. It is a value statement: "Buy this product, and you will get *this specific benefit*."

2. The proposition must be one that the competition either cannot, or does not, offer. It must be unique—either a uniqueness of the brand or a claim not otherwise made in that particular field of advertising.

3. The proposition must be so strong that it can move the mass millions, i.e., pull over new customers to your product. (Reeves, 1961, pp. 46–48)

The unique selling proposition is the implicit promise that you are providing to your clients, prospects, or potential employers (your "target") in exchange for them doing business with you or hiring or promoting you. But, do you know what your Unique Selling Proposition (USP) is?

Here are a few examples of commercial products that offered unique selling propositions:

- Head & Shoulders: "Gets rid of dandruff"

- Visine: "Gets the red out"

- Domino's Pizza: "Fresh, hot pizza delivered to your door in 30 minutes or less—or it's free"

- FedEx: "When your package absolutely, positively has to get there overnight"

- Kentucky Fried Chicken: "Finger lickin' good"

- M&Ms: "Milk chocolate that melts in your mouth, not in your hand"

A USP is a distinct idea that distinguishes you and your business from every other competitor. It is developed for each target market. It answers the question of "What value can you provide to your target that will help solve a problem, increase market share, or improve business, etc.?" You want to focus on that one niche, need, or gap that is lacking for your target, provided you can keep the promise you make.

EXERCISE

Develop your unique selling proposition.

Step 1: Identify your most compelling benefits.

With the needs of your target in mind, describe the three most compelling benefits you or your company can offer. Explain WHY this benefit is important to the target. Think about the result that your client (or potential employer) desires from you, your product, or your service.

_____

_____

_____

Step 2: What makes you (or your offer, product, or service) unique?

No two people have the exact same skills, experiences, or abilities. Therefore, there is a unique quality in your personal brand. It is your challenge to define it and package it for a target market (employer or client base).

_____

_____

_____

_____

Step 3: Solve a "pain point" for someone.

Before an interview, research the company and the industry to ensure that you understand what is causing pain for the target. Yes, pain! The key to marketing any product or service is to find a need and fill it; identify pain and provide a remedy. In the following examples, identify the pain point.

	USP	Pain Point
Head & Shoulders	"Gets rid of your dandruff"	Dandruff is socially unacceptable.
Visine	"Gets the red out"	
Domino's Pizza	"Fresh, hot pizza delivered to your door in 30 mi-nutes or less—or it's free"	
FedEx	"When your package abso-lutely, positively has to get there overnight"	
Kentucky Fried Chick-en	"Finger lickin' good"	
M&Ms	"Milk chocolate that melts in your mouth, not in your hand"	

Who are your targets and what causes them pain? How can you specifically address the targets' needs?

TARGET Example: Medium-sized consulting firms	Their Pain Point Newly recruited college graduates who dress like they are still on campus	Unique Selling Proposition Through my delivery style, I engage youthful audiences in creating a vision of themselves that supports the corporate image and I show them how to shop within a limited budget

Step 4: Prove it!

What evidence supports your claim that you can deliver on your unique selling proposition? Cite examples, stories, relevant experiences, and credentials.

Your Unique Selling Proposition	Proof Points

Step 5: Now develop a Yellow Pages ad that tells the story.

Review the previous pages. Start with your main target (you can develop several ads). First, write a statement that incorporates all of the elements (target, pain points, USP, and proof.)

> **Example:** For Baby Boomers who find themselves at mid-career (target) and in the midst of a career transition (pain point), I use my true-life experience of reinventing myself from a former engineer and mid-level utility executive to a certified image professional and brand coach (unique proof point) to demonstrate how developing personal branding strategies will help them get the jobs, secure the contracts, or elevate their visibility (USP).

Yellow Pages ad for Baby Boomer career transformation:

Baby Boomer Meets Personal Branding

> Marva Goldsmith can help you reinvent your career, because she has lived it! At age 42, she left a mid-level executive position in the utility industry to become a certified image professional, brand coach, and public speaker. Marva works with mid-career professionals to help them successfully brand themselves to compete for new jobs, new business and higher visibility.

Just as I used my experience to develop this "ad," you can use yours in any interview with a potential client or employer. You can also use variations of your USP in your marketing collateral, and, in some cases, a brief, toned-down version on your resume.

Use this exercise to develop your own "brand advertising" that will excite you and gain the interest of your target audience. Most importantly, a powerful USP will act as a compelling force to inspire consistent delivery on your brand promise.

_____

_____

_____

_____

_____

_____

_____

_____

CHAPTER 5

Branding: What It Is... and What It Ain't

Stake out your territory—
and clearly state your claim!

Ketchup

Tomatoes + spices + high fructose corn syrup = ketchup. Right? Pretty much. For the most part we can agree that all brands of ketchup are made of essentially the same ingredients. So, how does one brand distinguish itself from all the other ketchup bottles on the shelf?

Heinz captures more than 40% of the ketchup market by branding itself based on a single attribute: it's thick. What can we learn about branding ourselves, or our small businesses, from the Heinz ketchup example? Through several successful ad campaigns, Heinz has become known as the slow, thick, rich ketchup. Do you remember any of the following?

Tagline:	"Worth the Wait"
Ad copy:	"Slowest ketchup in the West"
	(See it on youtube.com)
Ad song:	"Anticipation" by Carly Simon

57

The packaging is now designed to accommodate this well-established attribute. Heinz changed the orientation of the bottle such that it is stored upside down. Still rich and thick, but now—no waiting.

Can you accept that in the workplace (or the market-place) you are no different than ketchup? No matter what you do—trainer, HR specialist, engineer, teacher—there are many other people who essentially do the same thing and have similar credentials (or ingredients) as you. So, what attributes make you different and special in your marketplace? Keep in mind that Heinz does not go after everyone who likes ketchup. Its target market is just those consumers who prefer thicker, heartier ketchup. If you like soupy or runny ketchup, you won't like Heinz.

It is important to understand that "distinguishing yourself" does not mean you are the only person in your organization, or marketplace, with these attributes. Heinz is not the only thick, hearty ketchup on the shelf. They were just the first to use this unique selling proposition, and now they have the brand distinction of being "the slow ketchup," or the "thicker ketchup." In branding yourself, you are simply pointing out how *you* want to be characterized.

What is personal branding?

We should start with a conversation about what personal branding is NOT.... I once ran across a great list on a website belonging to Tom Peters, who is credited with starting the phenomena of personal branding, with his article "The Brand Called YOU," which was featured in the magazine *Fast Company* in 1997.

The author of the annotated list is Rajesh Setty:

- **A PERSONAL BRAND IS** your promise to the market-place and the world. Everyone has a personal brand. The real question is whether someone's personal brand is powerful enough to be meaningful to the person and the marketplace.

- **IT'S NOT** what you say about yourself. Your personal brand is an assessment the marketplace makes about who you are and what you bring to the marketplace.

- **IT'S NOT** an extension of your employer's brand—unless you are self-employed.

- **IT'S NOT** your presence in social media. Social media can amplify your personal brand, but your presence there is not a substitute for a personal brand—unless you're a social media expert.

- **IT'S NOT** about the power alone. Power and influence are just possible side benefits of your personal brand. Personal branding is about what you can give to the world.

- **IT'S NOT** a gift that someone can give you. But they can give you a gift to amplify an "already powerful" personal brand—a well-deserved link, an endorsement, a testimonial, etc.

- **IT'S NOT** permanent. It's not something that you can get and keep it for life. Just as you must work hard to develop a powerful (intentional) personal brand, you have to continue to work hard at maintaining and growing that brand.

"Personal branding is an identity that stimulates precise, meaningful perceptions in its audience about the values and qualities the person stands for."
—Peter Montoya, author, personal branding expert

"Personal branding is [simply] a way to clarify and communicate what makes you different and special; then use those qualities to guide your business and career decisions."
—William Arruda, author, personal branding expert

We also learn from Heinz that we must establish a leadership role in our field. One of the most effective ways of strengthening a brand is to narrow the focus. **Think: Starbucks, Toys-R-Us, Subway.** No doubt there are hundreds of attributes you could use to describe You, Incorporated. To strengthen your brand, to distinguish yourself from all the other ketchup bottles on the shelf, you need to distill the list down into what you want to be a "top of mind" response when people think of you—your leadership role. For example: Volvo is described by two attributes safety and luxury. Heinz is the thicker, richer ketchup.

The most difficult part of personal branding is to identify your leadership role—what makes you different and special. The next exercise should help you articulate those distinguishing characteristics.

EXERCISE

Make four copies of this page. (Just this page, please-- you have my permission.) Circle all the attributes that describe you. Now distill the list into three attributes that you consider the most important. These are your key features.

Accessible	Helpful	Shy
Accurate	Honest	Spoiled
Active	Humorous	Spiritual
Aggressive	Imaginative	Stubborn
Aloof	Impatient	Successful
Arrogant	Insensitive	Supportive
Ambitious	Intelligent	Thoughtful
Analytical	Introverted	Tolerant
Assertive	Intense	Trusting
Beautiful	Inspiring	Unflappable
Bold	Intuitive	Versatile
Charismatic	Kind-hearted	Visionary
Cheerful	Likable	Witty
Collaborative	Loyal	Wise
Competitive	Loving	
Confident	Materialistic	_____
Conservative	Melodramatic	_____
Controlling	Moody	_____
Creative	Open-minded	_____
Dependable	Optimistic	
Detail oriented	Organized	
Diplomatic	Original	
Driven	Passionate	
Dramatic	Persuasive	
Efficient	Philanthropic	
Eloquent	Procrastinating	
Empathetic	Productive	
Energetic	Professional	
Entrepreneurial	Receptive	
Ethical	Relentless	
Extroverted	Resourceful	
Flexible	Responsive	
Forceful	Risk taking	
Friendly	Ruthless	
Generous	Sincere	
Healthy	Sophisticated	

I hope that you followed the instructions to make four copies of the previous page. Now, ask four trusted colleagues to circle up to six attributes that best describe you. (Sorry, we're working in the business domain, so you can't ask your mother—or your spouse.)

Write their responses in the chart on the next page. Circle any attribute cited by more than one person. The more circles you see, with the same or similar meaning, the better (assuming the items circled are attributes you *want* associated with your brand). That means you have at least been consistent in the image you project.

Underline any circled attributes that were on your list of key attributes. Ideally, your colleagues have written all or most of the attributes that you identified during your self-assessment.

What themes did your colleagues identify? Were there any surprises? Sometimes we find that we have to live up to our brand: people see attributes in us that we do not realize are present. Remember it's all about perception—and perception is reality!

If your colleagues picked different attributes from each other and from your self-assessment, you need to think about the consistency of your message. But don't worry: this is important information you can use to improve the branding of You, Incorporated. (Of course, you can contact MG&A for brand coaching, too.)

What distinguishes me from others in my field?

Colleague 1	Colleague 2	Colleague 3	Colleague 4

A simple way to brand yourself, whether you are an entrepreneur or an employee looking to rise above the fray, is to establish a leadership role in your field, gain visibility for the leadership role, and be consistent in your approach to deliver on your brand promise.

Dennis Rodman: A Unique Personal Brand

How do we create ourselves as a brand? Remember former NBA star Dennis Rodman? We can use him as an example of ingenious—and absolutely unique—personal branding. I have used the Rodman "brand" to demonstrate the power of personal branding in my workshops since 2005, because his brand is both unforgettable and highly visible brand. When he was just a nondescript 5'11 high school kid, Rodman didn't even play basketball, but after graduation he grew eight inches and joined a college team. Over the years he transformed himself, developing the Dennis Rodman brand into what his NBA.com bio calls "one of the most recognized athletes in the world...." Rodman was a defense superstar in the NBA for 14 years (NBA.com called him "arguably the best rebounding forward in NBA history"), but even people who care nothing about the sport often recognize his name and can usually tell you something about him.

What does that mean? It means that when we think of Dennis Rodman, there are two or three words (besides dominant rebounder and defender) that thousands of people associate with him: **Outrageous Bad Boy.**

Rodman and leadership

Rodman was a leader in his marketplace, the National Basketball Association—a rebounder who would stop at nothing to get the ball. He was arguably one of the best rebounders in the history of the game and he has five championship rings to back up the claim.

Rodman and visibility

What Rodman did brilliantly, and in a most unconventional way, was gain visibility. He started changing his appearance both on and off the court—constantly altering his hair color, flashing multiple tattoos, and displaying numerous body piercings. His metamorphosis from Dennis Rodman of the Detroit Pistons to Dennis Rodman of the Chicago Bulls was headline news on both the sports and entertainment pages. He became a celebrity and began to appear on talk shows—not because he was a fierce rebounder (although that helped), but because of his outrageous behavior and eccentric appearance. Being extreme is what made him different, notable, and very *special*.

Rodman and consistency

To brand yourself in a way that's understood by all, you must be consistent in your message. Rodman was consistent, both on the court as well as off the court. During the 90s when he was a part of the championship Pistons and championship Bulls teams, he became more infamous for his antics on and off the court than for his undeniable playing abilities. That was his goal and he was rewarded.

Ultimately, successful branding leads to a purchase or a decision. It certainly did in Rodman's case. He made movies, appeared on reality TV shows, and wrote two bestselling books. My favorite demonstration of brand strength is the commercial he made for milk producers. Wearing a milk mustache, and with his buff chest bared, Rodman sent a message without saying a word. Why would producers of such a wholesome product as milk hire Dennis Rodman? Because their message was clear: **Even Bad Boys Drink Milk!**

Although Rodman left professional basketball eight years ago, the Dennis Rodman brand continues to resurface, including when he appeared in the 2009 season of *Celebrity Apprentice*, a reality TV show produced by Donald Trump. Why Rodman, when he's no longer in the NBA? Because of his brand. The producers knew that Rodman, just by showing up, would boost the show's ratings.

Other successful personal brands

Love them or not, there are many historical and current examples of successful, powerful personal brands in business (Henry Ford, Bill Gates, Oprah, Warren Buffet), government (Franklin Roosevelt, Ronald Reagan, Barack Obama), and every other facet of life (from Mother Jones to Mother Teresa). It's not necessary to be outrageous, as Rodman is (that's *his* brand)—only to demonstrate what makes you different in your "marketplace." You must own a leadership role and be acknowledged for it. Gaining visibility for that role may be as simple as positioning yourself as an expert by writing a few articles, or maintaining a blog.

To craft your brand strategy, here are some key questions to consider:

How do you define your target market and what does the target care about?

_____

_____

_____

_____

How do you currently distinguish yourself in your marketplace? (If you don't know, ask two or three people who know you well.)

_____

_____

_____

_____

How do you demonstrate your abilities in the marketplace?

_____

_____

_____

_____

How do you make your special attributes apparent to your target market when you are delivering your products or services?

_____

_____

_____

_____

What are you doing currently to gain visibility for your leadership role? Or are you the best-kept secret in your marketplace?

_____

_____

_____

_____

Who are your brand builders? (These are the people who share word of your successes with others, or who help promote your brand.)

_____

_____

_____

_____

What recent successes do you need to be sure to share with your brand builders?

_____

_____

_____

_____

How are you consistent with the story you present in the marketplace?

_____

_____

_____

_____

What does your brand packaging tell the marketplace about what they can expect from your services or abilities? In other words, what story does your style of dress, your marketing collateral, or your center of operations tell about you and your business?

_____

_____

_____

_____

Coach's commentary: In your face!

Okay, moment of truth…did you read through the last segment of questions? You did notice the lines after each question, right? Oh, are you one of those people who watch the exercise or aerobics programs on TV while you sit in bed eating snacks and thinking, "I'll work out with them next time when I'm in the mood…"? Caught you! This is a **workbook**. Please go back and do the WORK!

You've done the work? Great, let's move on.

Taking charge of your personal brand

> *"Branding, by its very nature, is not optional.*
> *If you do not position yourself in people's minds,*
> *they will do it for you."*
> —*Peter Drucker, management consulting guru*

Do you *really* want to leave your brand to chance? Or do you instead want to take affirmative steps to ensure that the "space" you occupy in the minds of consumers is the positive one that you intend?

Here's what I know for sure—by age 50, you should be able to identify one or two attributes that distinguish you from others in your field. Even if you are changing careers, you certainly have talents that are leading you towards that future endeavor. Define your attributes and characteristics—how you want to be seen by others.

Let's review where we are so far:

- You've identified your "then" state by writing down the highlights of your last decade.

- You've identified what you want and captured your goals—in writing—for this personal branding exercise.

- You've conducted a SWOT analysis and taken inventory of the product—you!

- You are beginning to think about brand strategy, defining what makes you different and special, and making determinations about consistently communicating these attributes to others.

EXERCISE
With that said, what are you thinking? Get your thoughts and inspirations down now so that you can clear your head and make these thoughts work FOR you! C'mon, do a quick brain-drain...

_____

_____

_____

_____

_____

_____

_____

_____

_____

_____

_____

CHAPTER 6

Applying Branding Principles to Your Product—You!

Leadership

Leadership is about identifying what distinguishes you from others in your field. You have started that journey! You have identified your goal. You have conducted a SWOT analysis.

In every field or endeavor imaginable, there are opportunities to take a leadership role in your field of work. Identify what your leadership role will become in order to establish your niche. In Art's example, writing is his gift and passion, and he has experience as a publisher. His leadership role may be as a writer who can take you from thought to print.

Visibility

Who can you think of who already does what you love to do, and is successful at it? What is the difference between those people and you? Yes, you know about them, but do they know about you? That's important, too.

What have they done to become more visible? Where do you see them? Do they have websites? *Do you?* Are they associated with industries or trade organizations? *Are you?* How can you make your talent more visible with your target market—that is, in your field or within your company?

We are assuming that your skill set or quality of offerings are similar to those of the people who do what you want to do. If that is not the case, what do you need to do to get on par with your most visible competitor? You must have the courage to pursue your passion and then become known for it. If your work is not your passion, then how can you bring your passion to your work?

Consistency

Consistency is the keystone. Don't dabble in your gift, work with it like a hobby, and walk away. Ask yourself, "How can I build this into something that will grow and last?" The economic crisis certainly provides an impetus to turn your hobby into a viable business.

It's important for you to identify a leadership role and become good at delivering a consistent and quality product or service. That product or service can be delivered to clients or to your peers at work.

Branding occurs over time. That's true whether we are considering a commercial product or a person. The brand, "Marva Goldsmith, who delivers image and personal branding workshops and services," was born in 2001 and incorporated as a business on February 14, 2002. It has taken seven years to finally arrive at a point where my work is known in a niche of my desired marketplace. The community of people who know of my work continues to expand as a direct result of diligence in delivering a consistent service—and a strategic emphasis on visibility. In other words, I work at it, always.

For example, a part of my branding strategy is to become more visible to human resource professionals—people who are responsible for allocating the training budgets. I've begun to accomplish this goal by speaking at Society of Human Resource Management (SHRM) conferences. In 2005, I submitted a proposal to speak at the Maryland regional conference, but that first attempt was not successful. In 2007, I submitted a proposal to speak at the SHRM regional conference in New Jersey, and that effort *was* successful! I presented a workshop on Branding YOU, Inc.

I was then invited to present the workshop at the 2008 SHRM New York conference, and to expand my topic to "Branding You and HR." At this New York conference, I was a featured pre-conference presenter. That meant there were no concurrent workshops to compete against. Even better, this workshop was granted recertification credit status: participants received credit for attending.

After the New York SHRM workshop, I was invited to present in New Hampshire for their 2009 regional conference. With all of that experience and positive feedback to build upon, last year I also submitted a proposal to speak at the 2009 National SHRM Conference, to be held in New Orleans—the Mecca for HR professionals! Thousands attend from all over the country.

I am thrilled to report that I have been accepted! My 75-minute window of opportunity will occur on the first day of the conference at 7:00 a.m., so I'll be one of the very first people the "early-bird go-getters" hear from! Four years after my home state's conference rejection, I will speak at the national conference. Perseverance is crucial. And I haven't given up my goal of presenting in Maryland; I will reapply this year.

You should have two takeaways from this example: (1) branding happens over time, not overnight; and (2)

75

you must remain focused and consistent (a reasonable amount of persistence doesn't hurt, either).

So, you get the idea: leadership, visibility and consistency are critical components in developing a successful personal branding strategy, whether you are over 50 or not. If you have evidence that you have a good product—that you are a good product—make sure the marketplace knows about it.

Brand Strategy review

My goal: Increase corporate training contracts

My strategy:

- Demonstrate **LEADERSHIP** by delivering unique "value added" personal branding workshops.

- Increase **VISIBILITY** of my *Branding You* workshop within the HR community by speaking at SHRM conferences.

- Establish track record of delivering **CONSISTENT high-quality** workshops.

- Use conference evaluations to (a) show evidence of LEADERSHIP; (b) obtain more speaking engagements and thus increase VISIBILITY; and (c) demonstrate CONSISTENCY in delivery of a good product!

Ultimately, the goal of branding is for these efforts to result in a purchase or a decision...more contracts!

Getting visibility for your leadership role can be as simple as positioning yourself as an expert by writing an article, a book, or a blog.

Art re-visited

Art has a goal and he has conducted his SWOT analysis. Now, let's create a branding strategy for Art that will help him achieve his goals. This shows the process you'll want to use for yourself.

First, let's look at Art's strengths and determine the leadership role he will play in his chosen field so we can begin to craft a niche—a focused, targetable market—for Art. Having a niche does not preclude Art from taking on business outside that narrowly identified area. A niche simply helps channel limited resources towards gaining visibility and establishing a leadership role with a particular target market. Without a niche, there is no focus. Consequently, time and resources can be wasted spent chasing dollars. With niche marketing, it is more likely that the dollars will come to you. That's more like it, isn't it?

Art knows what he wants. **He wants to write.** That said, what type of writer does Art want to be known as? What leadership role does he take amongst the tens of thousands of people who, like Art, have a talent for writing? What makes Art different and special? These are the coach's notes that I used to prompt Art.

Art's Brand Strategy

Leadership: I want to establish a top-tier reputation for providing excellence and professionalism across a wide spectrum of written communication. I want to be a leader by providing solid, high-quality writing that effectively and succinctly interprets, refines, and sharply focuses my client's vision—that drives his or her point home with power and authority, that maximizes the message clearly, concisely, and profoundly. I want to succeed in furthering my client's mission.

Coach's query:

Art, what makes you different and special; what sets you apart from other writers and editors who want to provide excellent written communications that further their client's mission? How does your experience as a publisher enhance your role as a writer?

Art's answer:

I know the basic nuts and bolts of the publishing business, from editing through composition and manufacturing. I also know the more esoteric aspects of publishing, such as the labyrinth of copyrights, digital print-on-demand technology, CD/DVD duplication, artwork and design, and even dealing with overseas vendors and international shipping/freight forwarding companies. I also have a working understanding of postal regulations for mailing newsletters and journals (some print products will retain a raison d'être in the digital age!).

Visibility: I want to build and portray a high profile in the writing, publishing, and the broader information field as a solid, no-nonsense performer: highly efficient, intensely focused, and always on point. As a first priority, I plan to set-up a website that details the expertise I possess and the services I offer, to which I can refer prospective clients, especially on-line contacts. This website will emphasize just what makes me different and special. It will highlight my value proposition.

Coach's query:

What can your network of publishers provide you?

Art's answer:

I know enough people in the industry whereby a brief newsletter or blog (or a combination of the two) could be a very valuable tool. One problem is that most of my industry contacts are, or were, on the "back end" of the publishing process—typesetters, printers, digital replicators—the product "producers," in a word. However my target audience, at least at this formative stage, consists of the "front end" creators, writers, and editors of the content to be published. Thus, I will need to work on ways to recruit the help of my primary contacts to reach out to my target audience—which could be to their benefit, too. After all, a printer's representative might be very eager to put me in touch with prospective authors or editors if he or she thought it might lead to book manufacturing contracts in the future.

Coach's query:

Can you offer a bundled price? Or can you manage a project from start to finish...writing, copywriting, printing, etc. You know, "Hire Art Lizza: the NO-Hassle approach to writing?"

Art's answer:

There are groups and associations devoted to writing, publishing, and self-publishing, such as Para Publishing (and many others) that I need to investigate and consider joining. I will redouble my efforts in seeking out professional and trade organizations that will help me build that high profile visibility that I need to succeed.

I am interested in starting a "grassroots campaign" right here in my local community. I may be very surprised by the number of opportunities right in my own backyard. I believe I can get some inexpensive advertising through a host of local newspapers—the freebie papers we all get in the mail. I live in a mostly rural community with the usual sorts of local businesses that may need a writer, and I believe it is a community where it may be easy to establish a presence very quickly through a little advertising and *a lot* of word-of-mouth. Nothing fancy, no frills, no fads—just solid, reliable, and dependable performance. For example: "Need to make a case, or drive a point across with impact? Call Art."

Coach's query:

Art, now that you have considered leadership and visibility, you have to manage the delivery of your message to be sure it's consistent over time.

Most people miss this element of personal branding. Branding is not a one-step, simple process, like sending out an outstanding brochure or having a great logo and tagline. Instead, effective branding is achieved and nurtured by delivering a consistent experience that target customers have come to expect and rely upon, over time. And you must deliver on this promise each and every time.

Effective branding is the unwavering truth of who you are and what you represent in the marketplace—no matter the size of your market. What are the steps that you can take over time that will build your desired brand consistently?

Art's answer:

My professionalism and determination to do the job right and to get it done on time earned me a reputation for excellence, honesty, and cooperation on both the editorial and the publishing production sides. I was well respected by authors and industry insiders alike. The same type of dedication to excellence and to service will be critical to establishing a reputation for steady-handed consistency among my future clients. These traits (brand promises) will need to be used to the fullest extent possible in all of my promotional materials, both online and in print.

In short, I see no substitute for a measured, operational standard of excellence demonstrated over time—no substitute for hard work, and certainly no quick route to achieving the consistency goal. I'll have to earn it.

"Deliverables": a checklist of exactly what Art wants to establish (that is, his GOALS):

Leadership

- Establish a top-tier reputation for providing excellence and professionalism across a wide-spectrum of written communication

- Create communications that further a client's mission

- Capitalize on extensive publishing background and experience

Visibility

- Develop a website that emphasizes difference

- Develop a periodic newsletter for industry contacts

- Develop a blog

- Join writing, publishing, and self-publishing groups and associations

- Develop a "grassroots campaign" to become the writer of choice in the local business community

Consistency

- Deliver on time, every time

- Set a schedule for newsletter or blogging

- Identify two or three organizations to attend periodic meetings; consider a leadership role

Art has a great start on developing his goals. To make the goals more powerful, he will later develop a schedule for completing his goals.

A query for everyone: What if your goal is to find a position in the field of your choice and not to brand yourself in a new business role?

The simple process outlined in the last two chapters still applies to you. The good news is you are still narrowing your scope of desired employment by defining what you want. You will find that the SWOT analysis will be invaluable in helping you to identify the job or position that best suits your needs.

You will also discover that after thoughtfully completed the SWOT analysis, you will be able to handle any interview questions about your abilities or goals, because you have now studied you—the product.

- You will be able to define what distinguishes you from others.

- You will have your leadership qualities down cold and be able to discuss them flawlessly.

- You'll be able to identify opportunities to gain visibility for your leadership role.

- You'll be conscious of your brand promise and will know how to consistently deliver on it.

Prep work for any field you choose

Okay, what if you're not selling a talent, but instead have a talent for selling? Below is an example of a personal branding strategy to win a sales director's position.

Goal: Director of Sales

Target: Vice President Sales

Additional tactics can be added, but here are a few to get you started:

Leadership

- Distinguish yourself in the top tier of sales producers within your organization or industry.

Visibility

- Volunteer to provide sales training for new recruits or under-performers within the organization.

- Volunteer to create a sales "training tips" manual.

- Participate in formal management training programs and/or seminars.

Consistency

- Continue to deliver on top-tier performance numbers.

- Identify industry organizations that use your product and get active; participate in meetings, network, and/or take on a leadership position.

EXERCISE
Thoughts on applying these principles to your own
personal brand? Time for another quick brain-drain...

Leadership

_____

_____

_____

_____

_____

_____

_____

Visibility

_____

_____

_____

_____

_____

_____

_____

85

Consistency

_____

_____

_____

_____

_____

_____

_____

_____

CHAPTER 7

Passion and Branding

A passion for your brand—and turning your passion into a brand

In the first section of this book, I showed you the process of creating a brand strategy. In this next section we will drill down to mine your core interests.

COACH'S NUDGE:

If you are having trouble creating a brand strategy for yourself, take five minutes to clear your mind. Free your thoughts of daily stresses and mortgage payments and ask yourself, "What in life gives me the greatest pleasure?" Notice I didn't say anything about ways to earn money: don't filter your answer by factoring in possible sources of income. Just identify that one thing that makes you smile every single time you do it.

For me, this has always been shopping. For some, as with Art, it may be writing. For others, maybe it's painting, woodworking, talking to people, working with numbers, building things…you get the idea.

Now imagine combining your gifts with your passion. For example, if painting is your gift and nature is your passion, become known for creating master-pieces of landscaped beauty, or painting a series on endangered species.

WORKSHEET:

Create Your Brand Strategy

Using the answers to the questions posed in Chapter 5, define the following essential elements. (I told you we would use that information later.)

LEADERSHIP: How are you distinguishing yourself in your marketplace?

_____

_____

_____

_____

_____

_____

_____

_____

VISIBILITY: What are you doing to gain visibility for yourself in your leadership role?

_____

_____

_____

_____

_____

_____

_____

_____

CONSISTENCY: In what ways do you need to be consistent with the story you are presenting in the marketplace?

_____

_____

_____

_____

_____

_____

_____

CHAPTER 8

Sue's Story

Let's reinforce the lessons by example. Meet Sue
Thompson.

Then: Turning 40—An earthquake, a Master's degree, and creating a niche

In January 1994, right before the devastating earthquake
in Northridge, California, I was ready to tender my resignation from my disheartening, exhausting post as personal administrative assistant to a high-powered and
demanding university president. After the earthquake, I
decided to stay long enough regain my footing and then
move forward with my plan of becoming a mental
healthcare provider—only to have my life shaken up far
more during the following six months than it had been
during those 17 frightening seconds. I finally did leave
the president's office, negotiated a part-time role for myself at the university, and went back to school full-time.

At the end of 1996, the year I turned 40, I completed a
Master of Clinical Psychology at Antioch University in
Los Angeles. However, by the time I graduated and
completed my internship, I'd discovered that providing
therapy was not my thing after all.

I was disappointed by this discovery, but *not* with the
degree, although I wasn't sure how to use. I was sure

that I was sick of Los Angeles and wanted a change of seasons, a change of pace, and a change of life. I found a job posted on what was then the fledgling medium of the World Wide Web and ended up as the office manager for a small company in Delaware. My husband was waiting for a buy-out from a savings and loan that was changing hands, so we lived apart for a while, catching time together every couple of months when we traveled for business. We were childless, by choice, making this possible.

I took on more responsibilities at work, received training, and did whatever I knew I could do. I created a role for myself as the facility director, in charge of the building and its maintenance and functioning. I had found my niche! I worked with contractors, architects, and designers, and as a middle manager, I was in the perfect spot: I didn't have to participate in the big strategic decisions as a vice president would have to, but I executed orders well and liked being in command of those I managed.

How did I "create" a position for myself?

First, I knew my strengths and how they related to the needs of the customer—in this case, my employer. Second, I looked for ways to use my strengths in new ways. I knew I could be a great project manager because I have always been very organized and religiously thorough, but I didn't know how much I'd enjoy the design side of the work. Also, managing the care of the building fed my love of making people feel good about their environment.

In my late 40s, I got involved in some management initiatives and training that reignited my love of psychology, temperament studies, and personality development and rediscovered a talent I'd pushed to the back burner for a long time—public speaking. For years colleagues in professional organizations had asked me to

92

share my ideas at staff meetings and chapter events, and it finally became clear to me that I spoke with authority and that people perceived me to be an expert.

> **COACH'S TIP:**
>
> Other people can help you identify your strengths. Are you listening to them?

I took some motivational courses in public speaking and started making contacts, one of which resulted my writing and publishing *The Prodigal Brother: Making Peace with Your Parents, Your Past, and the Wayward One in Your Family*, which was published by Tyndale House in June 2005—the year before my 50th birthday.

www.amazon.com/Prodigal-Brother-Making-Parents-Wayward/dp/1589972597

When my husband finally came to Delaware, he could not find work in his field. He went through a serious depression, made worse by the fact that he hated Delaware.

Around this same time, I had taken on a really "Big Project": building my company's new, state-of-the-art, 75,000-square-foot, beautifully furnished and appointed office building, into which we were moving our 250-person workforce. With six months in preparation and another six months in construction and fit-out, it promised to be a fun project—and fun is what I'm all about! It would also provide an opportunity for me to use all of my talents, abilities, and recent training.

Or so I thought. Instead, I ran headlong into the worst experience of my working life. I thought dealing with the university president had been difficult, but managing the extreme behaviors of this company's president was like being hit by a bus. He was unhappy with his selection of our new location and was dealing with personal issues that I could not begin to fathom. He became psychotic. Yes, psychotic!

I received the brunt of his abuse. Every day was agony. I really can't exaggerate the enormity of the stress. There were times I would come home and retreat to my room to weep out the emotions I had not been free to express during the day. Still, something inside of me had sensed impending doom in the months leading up to the construction work, and I had already begun to prepare for this battle. Determined to make it through, as painful as it was, I knew there was something I was going to receive if I toughed it out.

I needed this resolve because I couldn't leave anyway. I was the breadwinner in my marriage. By the time the Big Project began, my husband had gotten his equilibrium back. Even better, throughout the long, sleepless nights of his depression, he'd taught himself complex graphics software programs and, lo and behold, he unearthed a beautiful talent! He'd begun a freelance business producing websites, newsletters, and promotional materials, but his work had not reached a place where it could support both of us. I had no alternative but to stay with the company. I had to complete this Big Project.

Had the company president been stable, I would have stayed there forever. Even in the darkest moments of the Big Project, I thoroughly enjoyed dealing with all of the players. Now, I may not be the world's best facility manager, but I am really good at understanding and appreciating the strengths of others and accepting their expertise. I know how to listen and make decisions based on what I've heard. I am openly grateful to people who help me and make me look good.

Even my immediate boss (who also suffered greatly during this project) would say dejectedly, "It doesn't have to be this way," as we both attempted to manage the president's irrationalities.

Finally the date for the open house arrived, where 200 people *ooohed* and *aaaahhhed* over the beauty of the place. The board members raved about the quality and the "wow factor" of the design. Yet, the president did not even mention my name. There was no acknowledgement at this open house of the work I had done. With the project complete, I retreated, exhausted, into a bubble. I believe I experienced a mild form of posttraumatic stress.

It took more than a year for me to regain some confidence and a little bit of drive. I turned 50 in 2006, and I wasn't sure what I was going to do next.

Turning 50—And rekindling my real passion

I was doing more speaking and gradually made that my focus. I went to seminars on how to build a consulting business, participated in teleseminars on various related topics, and read about others who had followed their leadings to do things that turned out to be timely and successful. My job as a facility manager was becoming less and less important to me, but my connection to my professional organization opened other doors. I spoke several times at the annual convention, presented at my local chapter, and wrote an article for the association's monthly journal.

I have become more comfortable with my style, which the father of psychoanalysis, Dr. Alfred Adler coined "life style." By "life style," Adler was referring to the approach people take to life and how their experiences lead them to adapt to their environment and create their own individual patterns. Those in my "style" category have the firmly held belief that we do our best when we follow our own instincts—what I call my "leadings." I have nothing to lose by following a lead or desire to find out if it takes me somewhere. More often than not, I have been met with marvelous opportunities and adventures.

I don't regret many things, but what I do regret is *not* doing what I should have done when I had the chance, or not realizing that I had the power to do something. I often tell people that hitting a brick wall on the path is a good thing; it informs you that the way you are going is *not the right* direction for you and that you should go a different way.

When I recognized how very possible it was to do what made my heart sing, to turn the activities that excited and energized me into a business, I followed the leading. I started with creating some great promotional materials, thanks to my husband, and taking the other needed steps to start a business.

COACH'S NOTE

Sue discovered a passion that was linked to her strength—public speaking—and then took action. Note that she also engaged in retooling.

Ministry and me

When I was much younger, I was a guest speaker in churches. I did this for a number of years and, in fact, I met my husband during one of my long stays in a town where I had ministered. I'm not an Evangelist; I'm more of a teacher, which is very common in the church circles where I held Bible-centered seminars and conferences.

I incorporated my ministry as People Set Free Ministries. Over those years, I occasionally spoke at women's retreats or church meetings. In 2005, when I was 49, a Christian publishing house released my book, *The Prodigal Brother.* To promote the book, I did numerous radio interviews throughout the country, wrote articles for magazines, and even participated in a television program that featured the book. My husband created a stunning multimedia CD that included me reading an excerpt of the book and telling of my ministry, and I sent it to 300 churches throughout the United States and Canada.

I thought the book was going to throw the doors wide open for me. I thought the ministry would explode with requests for speaking engagements and writings, but I did not receive one single request for my services. Not one! **NOT ONE.**

Can I explain to you how strange that was? I'd worked with other church speakers who had poorly designed websites, had not written a book, and who had mediocre or even poor presentation skills. Yet they had steady engagements and some even managed to support themselves with their ministry work. By contrast, I had this marvelous gift of having had a book published by a reputable house, and I had sent out a truly outstanding piece of promotional material to what was essentially my target market—and absolutely nothing happened. It was so odd and unexpected that I could not get upset about it. I just pondered the meaning. And then I had a dream.

In the dream, my husband married someone else while he was still married to me. (As dreams usually go, this made perfect sense. You know how weird they can be!) His other wife had a terminal illness, and my husband felt it was important that he be married to her for the remainder of her life. I accepted that, even though I was very sad. I love my husband deeply and can't imagine life without him, but in the dream he didn't belong to just me anymore. He might again someday, I told myself, but not now; I had to let him go.

I awoke with a profound sadness that clung to me for days. I ruminated upon that dream, rolling over the possible interpretations. I knew the dream meant something and I wanted to benefit from its wisdom. I talked to my pastor about it, and I told him I thought it might mean that I was supposed to put the ministry aside completely for now. At a time when the opportunities for my ministry should be popping up like daisies, my efforts were producing nothing, and it was time to let it go. Maybe the opportunity will return to me someday, I told him, but it's not mine right now.

What I was getting instead, I explained to my pastor, was requests for speaking engagements, and I had ideas that I wanted to pursue. I thought I could make a real go of the business, in ways I couldn't explain, I said, and thought it might be my true calling. I even had a name for it: "Set Free Life Seminars." I am all about the lessons of life and how they can set us free if we receive them in the right way. I speak with an authority that makes people want to listen to me. I have a joy that spills over and is invigorating and entertaining. I think this is what God wants me to do, I told my pastor.

He listened to me and helped confirm for me that I was traveling in the right direction. I established Set Free Life Seminars LLC. I started compiling my ideas. I took baby steps, feeling my way carefully, but determined to move forward.

A secular mission: weight reduction and control

To make my leap forward, I had to let go of some things that were important to me. I had put a lot of work into my ministry. My job was no longer fulfilling—and I was in the throes of menopause.

My worst menopause symptoms were hot flashes and a metabolism that dropped like a stone. It had never been great; I'd had a weight problem all of my life. I remember my mother lamenting over how fat I was when I was only eight years old. I weighed 150 pounds when I was in junior high school. In high school, I was the "fat girl" who never had a boyfriend. In all of my adult years, the

98

least I ever weighed was around 160, and that was a brief and shining moment. I had done the Cambridge Diet (the original liquid diet), the Cabbage Soup Diet, and most recently, the Atkins Diet. Atkins was great for me. My body actually does its best on a low-carb diet and I love all of the food I can eat on that plan. Earlier I'd lost 40 pounds, but had gained back 20 over the next couple of years.

I started following Atkins again, religiously, when I set up "Set Free Life Seminars," but this time, even Atkins stopped working, and my weight shot up to well above 200 pounds. I decided it was now or never. I could not stand in front of people with so much excess weight and talk about how great life could be. I made an initial goal of losing 20 pounds and followed the Weight Watcher's Points system like my life depended upon it. I had been exercising off and on, but I stepped it up and made sure I did some exercise every day.

I lost 21 pounds during the 10-week meeting cycle, and I was thrilled. I'm not one to need cheerleading when it comes to personal commitments, so I didn't sign up for the next round of meetings, but I kept up the program. It had not been difficult, and I thought I'd just keep it up as long as I could. My husband, the cook in our relationship, had gotten used to my needs and accommodated me with fantastic salads (which he also enjoyed!) and delicious preparations of chicken, fish and vegetables. I had everything I needed for success, so I thought, "Why not stick with it?"

A few months passed and another 20 pounds came off. I wasn't losing quickly—that's never happened for me. My body is as resistant to weight loss as they come—but I was losing consistently and I wasn't constantly feeling hungry.

My new business was growing. I was getting conference speaking engagements, some for a new lecture that I was very excited about: "Acting Like a Leader in a

Hostile Work Environment." I actually *had* learned something during my dark night of the Big Project and the ensuing difficulties with the company president, and I outlined the principles that had gotten me through. The presentation was an enormous success. People stood in line to talk with me, to cry on my shoulder as they told me of their own severe situations, and to tell me it was the best seminar of the conference. My evaluations were fantastic. I began to entertain the thought of writing a book on the subject and even started on a few chapters. It had become my next important thing, and I began looking for a book agent or an acquisitions editor.

These successes were accompanied by personal victories. More months went by, and more pounds came off. Now I was into an exercise routine that had me looking fit and feeling healthy. People were commenting on my weight loss every day. I had to buy new clothes and, oh my! I don't know why it was easy for me this time. This doesn't mean I didn't have days when I blew it or that I wasn't tempted at all.

The truth was that, somewhere along the line, food had ceased to be a huge issue for me. I didn't fight urges anymore; food was no longer my most important comforter. I didn't see my body as an enemy anymore, either. I had acknowledged early on that if I was going to lose, the weight was going to come off slowly because that's the way my body responds. I decided not to let it derail me, but to just stick with it as long as I could tolerate the deprivation. It turned out I didn't feel deprived at all. My husband's great cooking certainly had something to do with that!

It took me from March 2007 to roughly the time of my birthday in July of 2008—that's 15 or 16 months—to lose 75 pounds. Along the way I had to dedicate myself to a sincere lifestyle change, exercising *every single day*. I've done this occasionally throughout my life and have never maintained the effort, but now that I have decided

100

this is the way it's going to be, I can honestly say that when I am running, or working on my Total Gym, or doing Pilates, *I feel young!* I feel in control. I feel like my whole life is ahead of me and, of course, it is. We are living in a day and age when it is becoming more and more possible to live to 100 years old and still be in good health, if we make wise choices.

I still can't believe I've lost so much weight! I am in the 130s, way below the lowest weight I'd ever seen previously in my adult life. I probably last weighed what I do now when I was 12 years old. I wear a size 2! It feels like a release. It feels like losing the weight is a symbol of being set free. I am a living symbol.

I believe my new feelings about my body and my abilities are a leap into a new place. People talk a lot about "going to the next level," whatever they think that means, but they are terrified of the actual leap. I don't think we get to the next level by just walking up a couple of stairs; it takes a true act of faith to jump out into the darkness and reach for that which is ahead. So many get to the threshold and—no matter how ready they are, or how much talent and desire they have—they stop at that threshold and start telling themselves why they should *not* make the leap, at least not yet. Pretty soon they've backed away, losing the energy needed to propel them to the place that is waiting for them, ready for them—the place of expansion. I do not want to be 75 years old, or 85—or even 60—saying to myself, "I should have jumped. I wish I'd just throw caution to the wind. I should have done it."

> *"Sometimes you just have to take the leap,*
> *and grow your wings on the way down."*
> —*African proverb*

Sue's personal inventory

Relationship builder, seer (ability to identify talent and abilities in people), encourager, mystic with a ridiculous optimism about what is possible.

Sue's goal

I want to have a successful business that makes me available to people who desire to move forward and who need someone to show them the way—*their* way, not a canned or off-the-shelf way. I want to speak, write, and instruct. I want people to feel I gave them something they truly needed, even if they did not realize they needed it when they started their journey. I want to change lives.

I want to make enough money in my business that I don't need to worry about whether or not I can actually make enough money.

Sue's SWOT

STRENGTHS:

- Relationship builder

- Ability to identify talent and match people to assignments (understanding their strengths)

- Ridiculous demand for excellence. I subscribe to the mantra of Louis XIV, who made France synonymous with style and good taste: *Stick to the high end and forget the low. Never underestimate the importance of décor and ambiance.*[1] Do it beautifully and do it well. Proofread, proofread, and proofread. Write intelligently. Put thought and care into projects.

---

[1] Joan DeJean, *The Essence of Style: How the French Invented High Fashion, Fine Food, Chic Cafes, Style, Sophistication, and Glamour.* New York: Free Press, 2005.

Execute with style. Good design is good
marketing.

- Ease in front of groups

- Quick decision maker

- Love of learning and teaching

- Deep desire to see lives changed

WEAKNESSES:

- I can get very scared. I can second-guess myself
  ruthlessly.

- I have to fight against a fear of not having what I
  need to move forward (a particular degree,
  certain experiences, or a way of thinking).

- I am judgmental and critical. I'm impatient with
  people who don't share my standards for
  excellence. Sometimes I write them off. I do not
  like this about myself. I pray that I am successful
  at keeping it private, as I have no desire to
  offend anyone.

- I don't discipline myself in scheduling and
  meeting goals. I'm not always sure this is
  necessary, but if it is, I'm not good at it.

OPPORTUNITIES:

- I'm unafraid to go after knowledge I need. As
  always, I'll take every class, pursue new
  avenues, find the people who can offer what I'm
  missing, and storm heaven to fill in my gaps. I'm
  doing it now by pursuing high-end management
  consulting instruction because I believe I need to
  play with the big boys and girls.

- I believe the book I'm writing can be a
  bestseller. I believe it will truly help people and

they will buy it because they are desperate for answers.

- I believe people are beginning to become concerned about the importance of character and the lack of it in our society. This creates tremendous opportunities for me to be the character expert.

THREATS:

- Finances can constrain. It often takes money to make money, but I am only willing to increase my credit limit with MasterCard or Visa by so much. Excellence costs money. The training I need costs money. I need more money.

- Personal energy: I have to make sure I rest after completing big things. When I become depleted, I get angry and cranky and full of despair and self-doubt. This is when I always know I need a nap or a vacation, but the desire to push forward and skip those times of replenishment is huge. It's a constant struggle.

A conversation between Sue and Marva

Coach:

A couple of questions are still hanging out there for me. What is your position on the *Prodigal Son* book and your initial strategy to engage your target audience around that work?

Sue: When I had that dream, I felt it was a message for me to put that part of my life aside for now and go for the "secular" pursuit of my business. The book was heavily promoted for a good six months. Then I sent my mailing. I sold the book whenever I spoke in churches or at women's retreats. It just seemed to come to a slow stop. I finally came to believe that book was supposed to be written for—someone, maybe a few people? I don't know—who truly needed it.

Based on the parable Jesus told of the prodigal son, who demanded his inheritance from his father and then ran off and squandered it in wild living, the book is about the struggles of growing up. My parents devoted their entire lives to rescuing my alcoholic, drug-addicted brother, while I stood on the sidelines watching my family self-destruct. In the parable, the prodigal son comes home and the father, overjoyed, throws a huge party. His older son, frustrated and filled with resentment, tells him, "I stayed with you all these years and you never threw a party for me!" I saw myself as that older son, who simply needed acknowledgment that in the middle of all the chaos, he mattered.

I think this project will come back later for an "unveiling." It's in the background now.

Coach:

What was the product or service that was being offered to the churches? Are you totally abandoning this product/strategy? Is there a different target? Was there additional work done after the 300 church mailings? What was the outcome? Did you talk with the churches where you had conducted the seminars regarding the book and service offerings? What was their reason for not responding to your offer?

Sue: I didn't follow up. I was going to sit down and start making calls, but I seized up. I didn't know how to be comfortable promoting myself in that manner. I was still burned out from the job disaster. Then I gave that talk at the business conference and it started to turn my head toward the new speaking niche.

I'm still invited by churches as a guest speaker on various topics. I haven't abandoned it. I still receive calls for women's retreats and I'll do a Sunday morning service somewhere or a Wednesday night. Sometimes a three-night meeting on, say, how to know your gifts. Perhaps the activity of the ministry will come back to me again instead of merely being a side activity.

Coach:

I am interested in seeing you create a branding strategy around the book, since you have made this investment of time and resources, and the book has received high ratings. It just seems that there is more to be done with the book.

Sue: I prefer to look at my current market. Interestingly, though, my husband wants me to create a strategy around the book. He's already started on a website just for the book—and now you're saying this, too. Maybe it's something I should pay attention to.

COACH'S TIP

For VISIBILITY, offer a free book to the person whose birthday is closest to yours—so the audience knows you have books to sell—if you prefer a gentler approach than the more traditional hard sell.

CHAPTER 9

The Retreat

Crossroads at the Crossings: September 2008

As I mentioned at the beginning of the book, when I first considered what I would do for my 50th birthday, one idea was to treat myself to a spa retreat. I know it's just September and my birthday is not until December—but, I've decided to enjoy a significant event every month! **If not NOW, when?**

So, here I am at the Crossings in Austin, Texas. A time-out is warranted.

I'm here because I found a workshop that is so on-point that, if I didn't know better, I'd say someone ripped my brain open, read my thoughts, and designed it just for me. **It's for women in transition.**

I enter the gates of the Crossings. The adventure begins as I zigzag along the winding roads that lead to the reception house, sanctuary, spa and guesthouses. I pass robed guests who appear to be in some sort of transcendental state (apparently having just left the spa. Wow, can't wait for my treatment!). I venture out to the deck where I see others with nametags and recognize them as part of my group. Two lovely young women, Sara and Kathy, invite me to their table and we exchange pleasantries and pearls of wisdom. My 20 or so fellow participants come primarily from the Austin and Houston areas, one from Michigan, one from Phoenix and two from California; their ages range from 30 to 71, including a host of other mid-century divas.

With anticipation for tomorrow's activities, I retreat to my room for the night. It is nestled a short distance back, among beautiful shrubs, driftwood, cacti, and aloe vera plants meticulously arranged along the walking paths. I walk briskly, as the scenery seems ripe for a coyote or two to be hidden in the terrain, crouching and ready to strike!

The guest rooms are very nice, but spartan; there is no TV or Internet in my room. *I am aghast!* What the heck am I going to do for an outside connection with the rest of the world? Okay, relax…I can do this. There's Internet and TV in the public spaces, so I just have to make it until morning. I take a deep breath. *Maybe I really do need a time-out.* I did not leave my Black (*crack*) berry, or my laptop at home. In truth, that would *not* have been a peaceful experience—not for me.

My room has a Zen-like setting. I turn on the sleep machine that's situated next to my bed, tuning it to a classical music station (instead of the crickets or ocean sounds). It is lovely. As I type into my Internet-less laptop, I feel as if I'm playing along with the orchestra—the keyboard as my instrument, words are my notes—in harmony with the sounds I am hearing. I fall asleep listening to a beautiful symphony.

This retreat center is known for healthy exercise and food: yoga, meditation, massage, bean sprouts—that whole transcendental experience. I rise with the sun, (which is about 6:30 a.m. here), and reflect on life.

What is my intention for this weekend?

I intend to have a retreat experience that is rich and inspiring, with lasting effects. I hope to gain an insight or two that will lead me toward more fulfillment in my life. I plan to explore, to seek knowledge, **to stop wrestling with things I cannot control.**

First insights: Stop complaining about the things I can control and get into action; be happy in nothingness, recognizing that it alone is pure potential, and listen to the sound of silence.

What's clear is that I am grateful for my life. I know what I have is abundant and good, and enough in *this* moment.

> *"(A) rich person is not one who has the most,*
> *but is one who needs the least."*
> —*William Kroll, An Interview with God*

I have clarity of thought, creative spirit and the fortitude to continue to listen, to give, and to receive bountiful blessings.

From this space in time, I look back on a half-century of living and acknowledge that it has been good and I am well. Perfect? No; but, all is well.

In this space, I am open to new possibilities and in this **moment** I will create new possibilities. I'm able to move forward and accept that yesterday was just that, *yesterday*. And, that all my yesterdays are complete.

Given that I am turning 50, I thought this retreat would be all about me figuring out how to **BE** in this next phase in life and that it would offer a relaxing time to write this book.

The retreat, however, proves to be much more than that for me; it focuses on **self-care.** I guess that is how I want to BE in this next phase of life anyway, fully engaged while I ensure that I am taking care of *me* in a very special and complete way.

Keys to good health and well being

Self-care: Taking care of one's self. *"Oh, I already do that,"* you might say. Some people do, but what I discovered is that I am not one of those people.

Oh, I buy myself the pretty trinkets, treat myself to good meals, indulge in a quarterly housecleaning and great trips. But, then there are the fundamental missteps: I allowed myself to gain 20 pounds over the past five years; I exercise only once a week; I say mean things to myself; I do not meditate or attend a church service on a consistent basis. I also take on *way* too much, so I work 12 to 16 hours a day—*almost every day.* I don't connect with friends and family often enough (who am I kidding—there's no time.) *This does not constitute "taking care of me."* The only self-care that I provide consistently is mental self-care through continuous learning.

The retreat workshop focused on four key facets of a quality life: physical, mental, spiritual, and emotional development. As we 50-something attendees approach our Golden Age, there will be challenges and changes to encounter in each of these realms.

Here's what we are told:

PHYSICAL: Physical self-care is essential. Physical changes are apparent, but we can take steps now to nourish our bodies, through diet, exercise and rest.

While at the Crossings, I met other dynamic divas whose physical self-care has honored their bodies. Their bodies are toned. They are runners and marathoners; they have exercise routines and are conscious of what they eat.

EMOTIONAL: Emotional self-care involves being kind to ourselves, watching our internal "self-talk" and

110

our actions. Emotional self-care acknowledges the need for support, either through friends and family or through more formal support systems (e.g., therapists, coaches, career counselors, support groups, and, yes, **image consultants**.) I am so guilty of giving in to "being old" and actually speaking those words! Well, not anymore. **50 is NOT OLD!**

SPIRITUAL: Spiritual self-care may come through meditation, prayer, or communing with nature. You find guidance, direction, and support. Some find spiritual self-care by engaging in creative endeavors: playing music, drawing, writing, singing or dancing. I would also list massage in this area, as the massage that I received at the Crossings was truly a spiritual experience.

MENTAL: Mental self-care means stimulating the mind, whether through books, workshops, course work, or movies; we must stay tuned-up for the journey.

Are you taking good care of yourself? Are you in need of self-care? Are you creating balance in your life? **To find out more, visit reneetrudeau.com, or sign-up for her Self Renewal Retreats at the Crossings. *(Tell them Marva sent you.)***

The workshops offered at my September birthday retreat taught me that I must take time out, be in the present, give myself a break, and most importantly, create more balance in my life. I must learn to nurture my body and spirit; **especially in my 50s.**

I commit to establish new habits in my life, in each of these four key facets—starting NOW!

And you can too!

So, what's the connection between self-care and personal branding? No matter what you want to do, or how you want to be known, success requires operating at full throttle—looking good and feeling good. Even more importantly, in this new and rapidly changing market economy, we must create an environment, both internal and external, that is conducive to learning, thriving, and adapting. Focusing on and refining your brand identity will empower you in this process. And, let's face it the more you take care of yourself—get the rest you need, eat the foods that fuel the body, and exercise your body and your brain—the younger you look!

EXERCISE
Fill out the following chart:

- In the left column, identify your current level of self-care in each of the key areas.

- In the right column, describe in specific detail the new habits you will implement to better care for the brand you are launching.

Current State of Self-Care	New Empowering Habits
Mental	
Spiritual	
Emotional	
Physical	

Review

Let's review what you have accomplished thus far:

- **You've identified your THEN State,** describing the highlights of your last decade.

- **You've identified your GOAL,** what you want to achieve in this personal branding exercise.

- **You've conducted a SWOT analysis,** and taken inventory of the internal and external strengths and weaknesses of the product, YOU.

- **You've developed a BRAND strategy,** identifying how to strategically reach your goals: leadership, visibility, & consistency.

- **You've created a plan for SELF-CARE,** to nurture your mental, spiritual, emotional and physical self, in order to maximize your delivery.

COACH'S TIP:

This is a good time to check-in with a business associate—someone you trust. You may consider a friend or family member, but I suggest you first consult with someone who can give you objective feedback, within the context of your profession. Family and friends may root for you to stay "rooted" right where you are.

Peer review

Discuss your branding strategy with someone whose assessment will be completely objective and based on just the information provided—not someone who may be predisposed to an emotional or judgmental response to your decisions.

Family members may feel you're "throwing away" what Landmark Education terms your "probable-almost-certain-future." This is based on the presupposition that today and tomorrow will simply be a continuation of yesterday because you will not change. Those who are threatened by your desire to change— and those who are emotionally invested in the status quo—may not be the best people to help you sever the roots that confine you to your past patterns, enabling you to grow.

If you are reading this book as a part of a book club, partner with someone (or two) in the club to obtain this feedback. You may want to check back with this person (or persons) after you have completed this workbook.

Family Matters

When you have completed the WORK, which means you will have completed your NOW state and developed an action plan, you may *then* want to bring in your loved ones. Discuss your plan and get their input and support. Make sense?

Connect with Me

How are you doing? This may be a great time for you to check in with me or another coach. Take this moment to visit my blog at Branding50.com. Send a question, or make a comment. I would love to hear how you are progressing with this work. **Note: If you are reading this book in the year 2018, do not visit my blog—I'm now retired!**

Halfway Mark

You have completed the first half of the book. What have you learned about yourself?

_____

_____

_____

_____

_____

_____

What do you think about your possibilities?

_____

_____

_____

_____

_____

_____

CHAPTER 10

Reminiscing: Larry's Story

People my age (you know—50—a half century) do a lot of reminiscing. *You'll find this trip down memory lane to be worthwhile . . .*

It was the summer of 1981, June. We took a picture, just the four of us, standing together on the Michigan State University campus with our arms interlocked and big smiles beaming across our sun-kissed faces. The picture is as vivid in my mind as if it were taken yesterday. We each held one finger up *(the middle one)* in defiance; pointed in the direction of the place we had called home for the past five years, the Engineering building. **At last, we are rid of you!**

Michael (mechanical and electrical), Cloresa (civil), Larry (chemical), and I (electrical) took this one last picture in front of our "home" before we left to start our new lives.

I had not thought of that picture for years ... until I recently received an email from **Larry Scott!**

Thank goodness for Google! Larry looked me up and found my contact information. We talked for 90 minutes. It was as if there was no space or time between us—although a lifetime (or at least 27 years) had evolved.

Larry said he now lives in Honolulu. *I am not kidding: Honolulu.* We talked about families and grown children, divorces and old friends, and eventually our respective businesses.

Larry is 50 and in the midst of reinventing himself. I do not believe in coincidences. So, there is no doubt that Larry belongs in this book. I am happy my friend Larry has popped back into my life and grateful for the opportunity to engage with him in his reinvention journey.

Lawrence's story (He's still Larry to me!)

THEN: Larry's 40s—A leap of faith—and of location!

My "then" state starts at the age of 38, when I moved to Hawaii. That was the most pivotal transition point in my life. I was married (I'm now divorced) with two boys aged 8 and 5 when we moved to Honolulu. This move was based on faith; faith in God and my wife's faith in me. Hawaii was a dream, a place where people *wanted* to live, but, nobody *actually lived* in Hawaii. *Right?*

When we moved, I did not have a job waiting for me. We just cashed in our retirement and went for it. Although we had visited Hawaii before, this would be quite different. This time we were determined to stay—to take up residence! We did not know anybody. It would just be our family, a new frontier for each of us.

We arrived during the winter. *Did I mention that we had been living in metro Detroit?* Detroit had been good to me. I worked in the auto industry, at a sales job for a supplier, and I became pretty good at selling. My son attended school in Bloomfield Hills, a prestigious school district in Michigan. We owned a three-bedroom home in the suburbs with an in-ground swimming pool, on a two-acre lot. Yes, we were living the American dream, but we were not happy. So after having a wonderful time in Hawaii earlier in the year, my wife and I decided to go back, and this time, take the kids. It seemed from the moment we deplaned after our very long flight, our children blossomed and we accepted the blessings from this magnificent paradise. We could see and even feel that this would become our home.

Still, living in Hawaii was just a beautiful dream. Even though I looked for a job during that trip (and unknown to me, my wife had brought along our important papers just in case we needed to enroll the boys in school), nothing materialized. Every employer I talked to said, "People often say they want to live here, but most of the time they return to the mainland." This was the first time I had heard this expression of the "mainland" vs. "the island" and it really stuck with me. I was becoming a part of Hawaii.

We came to the conclusion that, unless I was lucky enough to be transferred to Hawaii (an extremely remote possibility), we would have to relocate there in order to make anything happen. So, we made the commitment and moved.

Living in paradise (almost)

A couple of months after we moved, I landed a job with a franchise of a national company. We found a very nice home, right next to Waikiki School, the elementary school the boys attended. The job was in air conditioning (A/C) sales. Although I did not know anything about A/C, my background in chemical sales allowed for a smooth transition. The pay was half of what I had been making back in Detroit, and the cost of living was at least 30% higher; but *we were living in Hawaii!* We were exactly where we wanted to be!

The plan was to live where we wanted to live, then everything else would follow. I believed this was the road to happiness and it has turned out to be true.

119

In Hawaii, the boys would be able to do the simple things that I was able to do as a child—normal stuff like going to the park unsupervised to play. I did not have to worry that they would become a statistic, devoured by the gangs or drug activity on the street corners. (This is not to say that this is the only life known in urban cities, but the prevalence of these dangers is much higher there than it is on the streets of Honolulu.)

Don't get me wrong, Honolulu is not perfect, but it is certainly close. The culture in Honolulu is that the people are friendly. They tend to view outsiders with caution, but once you are accepted it is "all good."

With my new job, I had some income and I knew my professional skills would eventually carry the day. My wife did not work. It was our original deal that she would raise our boys while I raised the money. So she was free to pursue her goals. Her ultimate goal was to eventually work outside the home, but she did not want to take an entry-level position. She has a marketing degree from the University of Detroit. So, she started her own business and I supported her decision to become a financial coach. Along with her, I started to learn more about stocks and option trading. I thought of my job mostly as a paycheck on my way to bigger and better things. I would put energy into making her business successful and thus we would be successful together. In the end, it did not work out, as she lacked the practical experience she needed to be successful. However, I learned a lot about the financial industry through this experience.

In my 40s, I had given up on the idea that a corporate job was the way to prosperity. There were fewer jobs available in Hawaii, especially for someone with my skill set, because there are very few chemical plants or large industrial users, the type of customers with whom I had always worked. My sales skills were still good. I could sell a product if I believed in it, so I was moving forward, albeit slowly.

Different industry, same politics

Then the air conditioning company made a significant change in our compensation structure. The sales force was to work on a commission-only basis. For my sales coworkers and I, this was a serious problem. No longer did we have the cushy existing accounts to fall back on—those accounts were given to office personnel instead. The commissioned sales force was now tasked with bringing in new business.

The market segment that I was calling on to develop new business—building owners—was really a different ballgame for me; however, this still fell right into my skill set. I can flat-out sell. The product was good, so I was well prepared and eager to take on this challenge. Unfortunately, I was unsure that my company would pay me as promised when the jobs started rolling in. I expressed this concern to my boss, who actually thought I was kidding. He said that getting a lot of new business was the last thing he was worried about, though they welcomed the possibility of significant sales growth.

I started to sell a lot of jobs. As I had feared, the company became uncomfortable paying me. I am a realist—I knew that corporate wanted the benefits of having me perform at my best, but I also knew they would never willingly want to compensate me properly for my stellar performance as they saw my commission mounting up. *(You would think that corporate would be happy, right? Doesn't it make sense that if I'm making money, they're making a whole lot more money?)*

The other salespeople, who were thrown to the wolves with the commission system, either quit or were eventually fired. One veteran salesman who had taught me a lot about the air conditioning business had a nervous breakdown and had to leave the company.

Even though the company was clearly doing better with a higher sales volume and increased profitability, it was clear that despite the company's verbal promises, my boss thought I was making too much money. I honestly felt my commission was well deserved and represented what I should have been earning in light of my contribution to the company's bottom line. It seemed like I had found my niche and this arrangement would have been wonderful as I moved toward my goal of financial independence.

Well, you probably know how this ends. Corporate wanted to move me back to a salary! Can you believe it? Oh, they did offer to pay more than I was making before the commission-only went into effect, but I was no longer willing to accept that. I began to plan my exit. I thought I would negotiate a buyout and move on. I would then trade options full-time and run my own financial business.

I'd been with the company for some time and was in the middle of a deal to sell a $1.3-million A/C project— the largest job of this kind ever to come out of the Honolulu office. My customer wanted to accept my proposal, but made a counteroffer wherein my company would have to carry the taxes, permit, and agree to pay $500 per day in liquidated damages if the plant was not finished on time. I knew where our competitor was with regard to price and terms (my sales skills at work). The competitor had bid the entire job at $975,000, and I told my boss that we were high by comparison.

My boss sat on the counteroffer until very close to the deadline. Then, against my better judgment, he required me to take a counter-counteroffer to the customer. This counter was to make them pay for the taxes and permit and extend the time period by one month before liquidated damages would take effect. Needless to say, the customer said "shove it" and went with the competitor's bid. We lost the job and I lost a large commission to boot. In the end, we lost a major project that would have made a good profit for the company.

As it turned out, the customer was quite dissatisfied with the competitor's work, so they did not end up satisfied. And you *know* I was not happy. Talk about the one that got away.

Even though this would have been the largest job undertaken by the Hawaii office, nobody other than my direct boss ever talked to me about this loss. The size of the project meant it had a lot of visibility throughout the corporation, and I have to believe my boss had to do a lot of damage control (probably blamed it on me.) However, I never heard a word about this missed opportunity from upper management.

This was the last straw for me. I decided I would take a buyout. I had been with them for 11 years, so I truly believed I had earned a severance package. I had another big project on the hook, so as soon as I obtained a commitment from the customer, I went to meet with my boss to let him know I was moving on. When I met with management, I presented the other big project—my parting gift. Not as big as the one they threw away, this one was only $900,000, but it would be very profitable for the company and a good commission check for me on the way out.

The meeting went poorly. After I presented the contract they asked me to leave—the company! They did not want to pay me for the new project and would not give me a buyout. Not quite the outcome I had imagined. They installed the job for this customer, but somehow did not believe they should pay me for my sales work.

Mind you, the company did not have access to this customer prior to my research and sales effort. How they could justify not paying me is mind-boggling. I understand I was an at-will employee, and they had the right to fire me, but to not pay me for my services was inappropriate. (I have since taken legal action for the commissions they owe me.)

The looming question was, *What should I do next, look for another job, maybe go back to the mainland?* Well I first thought I would become an options trader, and work from home. I thought I could become good at trading.

Then, one of my friends, who happened to be one of my best customers, suggested I start my own A/C business. He pointed out that I was well known and respected in town. He said I should not let my company push me out and that I should fight back, although I never felt "pushed out" since I had wanted to leave anyway. I considered the idea. I did have the skill set and connections, so maybe I should sell A/C systems on my own. My friend said he would provide me an opportunity to keep his company's business. So in February 2007, A/C Project Management, Inc., was born.

Turning 50: Larry's NOW state

Yes, I am 50. I have not said that very many times. Living in Honolulu, I feel as though I have lost track of time. The Hawaiian lifestyle keeps me very active, so I just don't feel 50. Or at least, I don't feel the way I have always imagined that 50 would feel. I don't feel 50 because 50 was always *old* to me—and, I am not old!

I have recently started to play basketball again, and golf as often as possible. When I'm on the court, I know I can't do the things I used to be able to do, but hey, I'm moving around. I am often running right by guys who are 20–25 years younger. They must not be very good players because when I was 25 years old, a 50-year-old guy wouldn't even think he could drive past me. It just would not happen!

Whether those younger guys are good players or not, or whether it's just a matter of my competitive nature, I'm happy I can still play, and happier still that this does not square with my vision of being 50 years old.

My birthday falls on the Fourth of July, but I did not celebrate my 50th in any special way. This gift of living 50 years has changed me. I know I'm not a young man any longer. I embrace my role as the dad of two young men and this has been a great time in our relationships.

"Brand Larry": The promise and challenges of entrepreneurship

LEADERSHIP: Professional Strengths

It is something of an ironic footnote to my story that in the months since I struck out on my own, I've had quite a number of employment offers from large corporate suppliers. Now there's a group that doesn't seem to care that I'm 50! I could certainly do the jobs they are offering, and do them very well, but I'm past that now. I have too much to offer elsewhere. I could mentor young people who are just getting started in the business, design sales/marketing plans to maximize business penetration to meet today's challenges, and yes, I could sell products and services directly—I've already proven that.

At the age of 48, I started a new life as a business owner. The biggest change for me is that I'm doing only the things I want to do and the tasks that I believe are important. This business is an extension of me.

The "green" trend has become front-and-center in Hawaii, as well as across the country. The average electric rate in Honolulu is about $0.31 per kilowatt-hour (kWh), and on the outer islands it is well over $0.50 per kWh. When I first opened my business, I was primarily focused on air conditioning hardware, equipment, and installation, until I realized people were really beginning to talk about saving money on their electric bills and reducing the stress we put on this planet due to our energy consumption. As you no doubt have guessed, these days

I am talking a lot more about saving energy and crafting my product and services mix to meet the demands and desires of my customers to do so as well.

VISIBILITY: Seizing Opportunities

I'm a board member for the Hawaii Building Engineers Association (HBEA). This organization has provided me with the opportunity to give back to the engineering community which includes degreed, professional and operating engineers—the men and women charged with running the high rise office buildings, hospitals, and universities in Hawaii.

We are here to improve the quality performance of the building engineers in Hawaii. Our focus is to provide building engineers with the educational, networking, and "second opinion" resources that help them to be successful in their positions. HBEA accomplishes this goal through its quarterly meetings, through presentations on products and services, and finally by providing training classes on building and engineering basics. These varied classes include such topics as math for engineers, basic electricity, air conditioning fundamentals, and building systems for property managers. This has been a great way for me to stay connected to my market. It also provides a forum for me to give presentations on timely subjects, as well as updates on A/C Project Management, Inc., services.

CONSISTENCY: Performance Strength

All projects are handled with the customer *always* in mind. We make sure we provide quality—not just conformance to requirements, but real quality. When our jobs are complete, they work as advertised. They also have what my friend calls the WOW factor. Now, I do not know if this is original, but I describe the WOW factor as, "I know it when I see it." Customers know it when they see it too. The jobs look good, the customers feel great about the decision to hire me, and they just exclaim, "WOW!"

Our job is going to look good. The customer's space is going to be neat and clean. If we scrape a wall, we paint it; if we rip a carpet, we repair it. We leave the job site always in at least the same condition as before. I want people to know that we were there, that everything works and that everything looks good. That's what I mean by the "WOW factor!"

I *really* hope I never have to eat these words: *I'll never go back to a corporate job—I know a much better way now.* While my desire to never have to go back to corporate does put some real pressure on me, I can also use it as a source of motivation. I also feel that I must be successful because I don't want to go backwards. I want to move forward. Success, therefore, is the only acceptable option for me. As much as the corporate option will be out there for me, should I ever want it, there is really no doubt in my mind that it would make me a less positive person and a lot less happy. Now that is something that would actually make me feel old!

ATTRIBUTES: Resilient, malleable, caring, customer-focused, relationship-driven, knowledgeable, harmonious, and earth-conscious

Larry's branding strategy

LEADERSHIP NICHE: To provide essential air conditioning installation and maintenance service to business owners on the Hawaiian Islands while teaching clients how to save energy.

VISIBILITY: Maintain visible role in industry association as leader, mentor, and presenter.

CONSISTENCY: Develop consistent messaging for the target market through marketing collateral. Develop periodic opportunities to teach and/or mentor young engineers. Consistently deliver WOW!

COACH'S NOTES:

Lawrence used a brilliant strategy! What's so great about his involvement in HBEA is the genuine way in which he approaches his participation; he wants to help others gain knowledge and support the development of the A/C industry in Hawaii.

His focus on teaching and mentoring others will assist him in being known for his experience and professionalism, most likely resulting in partnership opportunities with others in the A/C industry. Lawrence's knowledge and customer focus will help maintain customer loyalty and provide opportunities for additional word-of-mouth advertising.

To be considered a leader, there must be confirmation or evidence of the claim of leadership. For example, if you own a restaurant and you claim that it serves the best food in town, evidence that you are a leader in your field would be critical acclaim in the media, long lines, or difficulty obtaining a reservation. In Larry's case, customer testimonials provide evidence of his ability to deliver the WOW factor.

Using testimonials and letters of recommendation help build brand awareness. Lawrence will continue to obtain testimonials for use in his marketing collateral and web site. Next steps for Lawrence are to differentiate A/C

Project Management as an environmentally conscious air conditioning provider and develop marketing collateral and a website that carries these messages.

To clearly draw that picture, Lawrence will need to capture evidence that his customers are enjoying the benefits of his work (A/C installation and services) and documenting the customers' energy savings through other measures.

Collateral development: initial steps

As a first step MG&A conducted a survey to gather customer feedback (see comments on previous pages). We then developed a tagline that captures the leadership role that A/C Project Management will pursue: "Connecting Energy and Environment."

We created a business card that begins to provide a brand identity for A/C Project Management, and there are plans to develop a brochure to assist Lawrence in articulating what the company stands for and their brand promise of delivering WOW customer service (supported by customer testimonials).

What about your business? Are you ready to invest in the image of your company?

Questions to consider that will help you understand what message your marketing collateral might be sending to your clients about your business.

Is your business email address associated with a free consumer account (gmail, hotmail, yahoo)? If so, what message are you sending to potential customers about your investment in your company?

_____

_____

_____

_____

Are the materials that represent your company printed on your desktop printer with perforated edges to tear off, giving the message that you just opened your company yesterday?

_____

_____

_____

_____

**Does your material clearly state what makes you
different or special—your niche—or is it so generic that
it could apply to almost any business in your industry?**

_____

_____

_____

_____

**What evidence of excellence (e.g., testimonials,
awards) are you relaying to potential customers?**

_____

_____

_____

_____

CHAPTER 11

Lessons From Dolly: Your Package

What we can learn about image from DOLLY?

Beautiful and vivacious, she is known for her curvaceous body and her beautiful voice. I recently watched the icon on *The Tonight Show*. As she sat talking with Jay Leno, I was surprised—as I am sure other viewers were—to hear that she was 62 years old. **Wow! She looked great!**

That is, until she stood up to sing. With a skirt that was four to five inches above her knee, she aged 10 years by merely standing up and revealing an unflattering feature. I found myself reducing my assessment to "she looks great for a 62-year-old woman."

Why the change in my opinion? When you dress like a younger woman, you position yourself to be compared to younger women. She had great legs for a 62-year-old woman, but carries the telltale signs of age—knobby knees!

There are many fabulous books on dressing well at any age. I will not attempt to replicate their advice, but I have listed a couple of ideas for over-50 job seekers. When in doubt, seek the advice of a professional.

Your packaging helps define the message you send to others

Companies spend millions of dollars packaging their products to ensure that their message is apparent. (It shouldn't cost you nearly that much!) Look around the house at products you have purchased, paying attention to the packaging. Ivory Soap and Campbell's have distinctive packaging. Like most products, you should be distinctively packaged, too. But, what does your packaging tell consumers about the product? Are you a trusted, familiar, reliable stand-by, or a fresh, innovative breath of fresh air? Are you a classic or unpredictable? Do you project confidence and competence or uncertainty and indifference?

What does your packaging look like?

Some think of image as something shallow or relating only to surface features, but as with commercial brands, personal branding includes the proper selection and construction of your personal brand packaging.

First impressions matter. You must take control of your appearance. People form opinions of you—right or wrong—within moments of meeting you. That means you can't afford to leave someone's impression of you up to chance.

Studies show that in the first 30 seconds of meeting you, people base their impression of you on this:

55%	**What they see**
38%	**How you speak**
7%	**What you say**

We all know snap judgments can be wrong and unfair. Still, you can't ignore the reality: people form opinions based on the most minor details. More than half of what goes into forming someone's first impression of you happens even before you open your mouth. That's right: 55% of someone's initial response to you is based on visual cues. That could easily be a whole workbook in itself (check out *Spin Me: Creating the Image That Gets the Job; An Image Guide for Recent Grads and Job Hunters*), but for the basics, here's a primer on what to consider, especially when going to an interview.

Clothing—People do judge books by their covers, every day. Make sure that *your* cover conveys the message you want people to remember. Here's a sample of messages that your clothing might be saying about you (whether you like it or not):

Tips for the 50+ job seeker

> *You can't help getting older, but*
> *you don't have to get old."*
> —*George Burns, Comedian*

- First and foremost, if you purchased your interview suit in the 1900s…think about an upgrade. You must look current. Your clothing, your eyewear, and your hair must tell the story that you are current. That does not mean to dress like a youngster, only that you must appear up-to-date, interesting, fresh, competent, etc. Invest in an all-weather wool suit in navy blue or charcoal gray. For creative industries, you have more latitude with color.

- *Both sexes:* Make a statement about your personality with your tie or scarf choice and/or jewelry selection. For men, think of the tie as a highway to your face. What highway is the interviewer on? Interstate (I)-boring or, I-interesting, I-creative? The tie should have a fairly small pattern so that it remains somewhat conservative; use color to tell the story. Women especially can use jewelry to bring color and interest into the interview uniform. Earrings should not dangle and the jewelry should not make noise, as it can be distracting.

- *Both sexes:* If your hair is silver, wear accents of blue or a French blue shirt to add vitality to your face. Depending on your personal coloring, a white shirt can drain the color from your face, leaving a "ghastly" appearance. If you have stark silver in your hair (and the rest of your hair is black or very deep brown—avoid brown tones; the color will make your hair look dull.

- *Both sexes:* Before your interview, use Visine. Not only does it get the "red out," it also whitens and adds a little sparkle.

- *Both sexes:* If your teeth are stained, consider professional teeth cleaning or whitening. If that's too expensive, then opt for some of the over-the-counter toothpaste whiteners.

- *Women:* Please do not wear a skirt that is above your knees to an interview. Remember, most interviews are conducted sitting down—usually without a table in front of you. When you sit, your skirt rises. The perfect length is mid-knee or, if you still have killer legs, at or just above the knee. But test it first: sit down to see how much leg is exposed to your interviewer.

- *Women:* Make sure your undergarments fit properly—no VSB (visible panty lines) and a well fitted bra can take years off of your appearance—especially the latter. Consider a body shaper to eliminate muffin top and help correct your posture.

- *Both sexes:* Keep perfume, cologne, and aftershave to a minimum. You don't want to overpower your interviewer. Consider a fresh, light, and airy scent for daytime, or nothing at all, in case your interviewer is sensitive to scent.

- *Both sexes:* Make sure that your nails are well manicured. Apply a good moisturizer on the day of the interview to minimize lines and any blotchiness.

- *Women:* Do not wear bright red lipstick to an interview; tone it down for the day. High-contrast colors will bring more attention to age lines around your lips.

- *Both sexes:* Your shoes should be polished, well-heeled and easy to walk in. Avoid thick rubber soles (of the orthopedic variety—unless you need them), and stilettos (just let it go).

Speaking Style

If you doubt that the power and quality of a voice can make a difference in the image you project, think about James Earl Jones. What's the first thing you think of? Though he is a fine actor with a commanding presence, his greatest asset is that rich and resonant bass voice. (His voice has been immortalized as the character Darth Vadar in the science fiction *Star Wars* franchise.) Not everyone has such a gift. **But everyone can work with**

what they have. Use your natural voice, speaking at a normal rate and volume without punctuating your sentences with sighs and filler sounds (e.g., um, well). Vary your intonations: modulations convey your enthusiasm, interest, and comfort with the subject. Pay attention to vocal inflection (you don't want to put anyone to sleep), use clear pronunciation and enunciation, and if you have a phrase that you tend to repeat (e.g., in fact, to tell the truth) try to shake the habit.

Body Language

Start with a firm, sincere handshake, maintain eye contact and give a warm smile. The handshake is critical because it initiates the social contract. Whether you are going to the most important meeting of your career or not, you should come across as confident and capable. Don't stare at your shoes or, even worse, into space. Don't fidget with your hands or hide them in pockets or behind your back. **Enter the room with poise, confidence and a self-assured presence, as if the cameras were rolling and you're the star.** Once you sit down, try to appear relaxed, but don't go to extremes: no lounging back in your chair or slouching.

CHAPTER 12

Vision—A Gift...and a Curse

A Book In Four Chapters

Chapter One: Once upon a time there was a boy who walked down a street and fell into a manhole.

Chapter Two: The boy walked down the same street, saw the manhole, yet fell in again.

Chapter Three: The boy walked down the same street, saw the manhole, and walked around it.

Chapter Four: The boy walked down a different street.

I don't know who wrote that "short book" with the big lesson, but its message is clear. You may easily "see" an obstacle or opportunity, but it's another thing to internalize the information and act upon it.

Exploring your vision: It's a gift and a curse

Let's explore the question of your VISION, the ideal state you are working toward creating. If you are like most ambitious people, you are always on the move, always in pursuit of the next thing. You're moving fast and are almost always focused on the future, sometimes to a very intense degree. You barely stand still long enough to take a snapshot of your current state. That makes pinning down and defining your "vision" difficult. As the obsessive-compulsive TV detective Adrian Monk says of his incomparable powers of logic and deduction, for example, "It's a gift...and a curse."

EXERCISE
Write about your future as your present reality.

Let's try your vision on for size—— give it a test drive. To do so, you'll write your vision statement in the present tense. **It should not be your current life, but your vision for your future, written as if it were true today.** We are declaring the future as if it were **NOW!** Let's make it clear. How do you get from THEN to NOW? Vision and ACTION!

When I think of a clear vision statement, I think of Pepsi. For Pepsi, the statement "Beat Coke" creates a compelling view of the future. It is clear and concise. It does not leave much to the imagination. Anyone on the Pepsi sales and marketing team understands the vision of the organization. Simply put, Pepsi wants to oust the number one cola brand, Coca-Cola, and take the number one spot.

If your goal is to find a new position or start a business, and you don't have a compelling vision of where you are going, it will be difficult to line up the resources, organize your strategy, or make your goal become a reality. Once you place the stake in the ground everything you do can then be in alignment with that vision. Writing your vision, NOW, puts your stake in the ground.

140

In December 2005, after 108 years of competing, the PepsiCo brand finally beat Coke!

So, how does this information apply to your branding efforts? With any product, including ourselves, the more clearly we can summarize our goals for the future, the easier it is to craft a strategy that will enable us to begin realizing that vision.

Now, we certainly intend to reach our vision—or at least move in the direction of the vision—in less than 108 years. The point is to have a vision and then place resources and action in alignment with that vision.

> *"Vision is the art of seeing the invisible."*
> *—Jonathan Swift*

Marva's vision for NOW

I defined what I want: To be free. Here's how my own VISION statement will help me achieve that goal.

- My e-books and products have sold more than 100,000 units every year since 2009, bringing me financial freedom.

- I have a national nonprofit organization, UXsformU, which employs at-risk and formerly incarcerated youth, giving them a fresh start, a brighter vision, and a healthy love of self. We are transforming lives. This brings me joy, which feels like emotional freedom.

- I have finally figured out how to successfully combine work and play. My speaking and consulting engagements include some of the best resorts in the world: Hawaii, France, Brazil. Yes, I get paid well—while on vacation. I work ten hours a month and play (or network) the rest of the time.

- I am a mentor to small business owners, as well as family members and friends who are starting or have started businesses. I am respected, appreciated, and fulfilled.

- In my personal life, I am balanced. I am taking care of myself in all aspects of my life: physical, spiritual, mental and emotional. And by the way...I am no longer single.

What is your vision for your present NOW?

_____

_____

_____

_____

_____

_____

_____

_____

_____

_____

_____

**Write your vision—your goals—as if it were your
present reality.**

_____

_____

_____

_____

_____

_____

_____

_____

_____

_____

_____

_____

_____

_____

_____

_____

_____

*"Don't underestimate the power of a vision. McDonald's
founder Ray Kroc pictured his empire long before it existed,
and he saw how to get there. He invented the company
motto—'Quality, service, cleanliness and value' and kept
repeating it to employees for the rest of his life."*
—Kenneth Labich, Business Guru

*"Peak performers want more than merely to
win the next game. They see all the way to the championship.
They have a long-range goal that inspires commitment and
action."*
—Charles Garfield, Peak Performer

CHAPTER 13

You Can't Get from THEN to NOW Without ACTION

October 13, 2008

As you know, I promised myself that I would do something significant each month until my December birthday. In October, I made a significant purchase. It cost $3,000.

His name is Adam.

Now, before your mind starts to wander in the wrong direction, Adam is a branding expert who focuses on media. For my budget, Adam represents a very healthy investment—one that demonstrates my commitment to achieving my NOW state.

How committed are you to your vision? How much are you willing to invest to make it happen?

Many people will read this workbook. Some will complete the exercises, others may even feel motivated to pursue a new career or start a business and make plans to go into action. But only a precious few will actually put resources behind their plans and take the first steps toward realizing their vision. **You can't get from THEN to NOW without ACTION!**

My pet rock—make that e-rock!

As a baby boomer and entrepreneur, I have high regard for Gary Dahl, the inventor of the Pet Rock. The Pet Rock was a plain old rock, nothing special—until it was marketed as a pet. It was sold in a cardboard box that looked like a pet carrying case. It contained a training manual with topics like, "How to House-train your Pet Rock." The rock, which sold in the 70s for $3.95, was featured in *Newsweek*, sold in outlets all over the country, including Neiman Marcus, and eventually earned Dahl a coveted spot on *The Tonight Show* with Johnny Carson. For me, the success of the Pet Rock is a constant reminder that all things are possible.

One facet of my NOW vision state is to become an Internet millionaire. The Internet is the only vehicle I know of that, with a good product and proper marketing strategy, can help you create wealth literally overnight. *Can I sell 100,000 units each year at a profit margin of $10 a piece on the Internet?*

By accomplishing this goal, I will then have the capital to fund my nonprofit, and spend my Golden Years experiencing the world...*Free to roam the country.*

The single-subject SWOT

Since I have asked you to conduct a SWOT, I will share the Single Subject SWOT that I wrote for this one goal: becoming an Internet millionaire.

Strengths

Over the past seven years, I have written five unique workbooks:

- ***I Don't Need No Manners, 'Cause I Live in the Hood!*** *(It's Not What You Think; the Hood is a State of Mind!)*

- ***Spin Me: Creating the Image that Gets the Job:*** *An Image Guide for Recent Grads and Job Hunters*

- ***Marketing Yourself For The Future:*** *A Career Exploration Workbook*

- ***Branding You, Incorporated:*** *A Guide to Creating and Maintaining Your Personal Brand*

- ***The Civility Playbook:*** *Avoiding the Personal Fouls in Life that Can Get You Thrown Out of the Game*

To see more, please v*isit marvagoldsmith.com.***

I am blessed with an active and creative spirit and a deep desire to be a catalyst for change in the lives of others. Feedback forms demonstrate that my workshops are transformational for many who participate.

I trust *and follow* my intuition. I firmly believe in the power of group genius and I continue to enlarge my circle of creative spirits, often enlisting them in the work of MG&A. So, I should always have plenty of meaty content to sell on the Internet.

Weaknesses

I am content driven. I love the act of creation. The older I become the more introverted I am. Introversion is not a bad thing--it just means that I enjoy the quiet, thoughtful practice of creation. I am often slow to go to market and I prefer a word-of-mouth sales technique.

Is this working for me? I've been successfully self-employed for seven years, but I have not realized my full potential, and I do not believe I can reach my goal of becoming an Internet millionaire without an intervention, which is where Adam comes into the picture.

Opportunities: Adam and other collaborations

Adam, my branding expert, is pushing me to move outside of my comfort zone. We are recording some short vignettes for Internet use and possibly a radio campaign focused on the "Marketing Yourself for the Future" workshop and workbook—tools designed to assist people as they navigate the rough terrain of career reinvention. Our advertising strategy will be as aggressive as my budget will allow, coupled with a grassroots public relations campaign to capitalize on free advertising.

In addition, I am teaming with Detroit-based midlife makeover coach Karen Batchelor, who also reinvented herself after the age of 50. She enjoyed an illustrious career as an attorney and community affairs executive. Karen is now known as a midlife muse and career reinvention coach. Visit her website: karenbatchelor.com.

Karen and I teamed with Baltimore-based financial planning guru Phil Dyer to create a webinar and toolkit that will combine our strengths.

Visit our website: tufftimestoolkit.com. Karen, Phil and I will target mid-career employees who are in transition during these tough economic times.

Part of my Internet strategy is to develop "widgets" for several of my e-books to enable sales by others in the "reinvention" industry on their websites. They will receive a percentage of sales and I will have a new avenue for promotion and distribution.

If you are interested in carrying this e-book on your website, email me: marva@marvagoldsmith.com. I will also market the book to book clubs and coaching circles, like the Five O'clock Club.

Threats

The **law of diminishing returns** states: "When you apply fixed and variable inputs beyond a point or limit, the outcome will be less and less utility with each additional unit." Simply put, I can continue to create products and workshop content, but without a significant change in marketing strategy, my success will be limited by my ability to market those products. So I can work harder and harder, but without an effective marketing strategy and resources to implement the strategy, increased work will not result in a proportional increase in productivity or income.

As you can see, the Single Subject SWOT does not have to be long or laborious. It helps you focus. What's clear to me is that I need to enlist others in my work, especially in the area of promotion and sales.

Now it is your turn to conduct a Single Subject SWOT. Get in the habit of conducting a quick SWOT analysis for your important goals.

Your SWOT Goal: _____

Strengths

_____

_____

_____

_____

_____

_____

_____

Weaknesses

_____

_____

_____

_____

_____

_____

_____

Opportunities

_____

_____

_____

_____

_____

_____

_____

_____

Threats

_____

_____

_____

_____

_____

_____

_____

_____

November 1, 2008

My November birthday gift will not cost me anything. This month I will spend time renewing relationships, putting people first, and just enjoying the journey.

What a gift!

CHAPTER 14

Ready, Camera, ACTION!

Power-filled actions!

So, this is it! When it comes down to it, it's all about action.

In a second you can take charge, develop a new path, and create a new chapter. Plan to accomplish some small feat every day. By the end of the month, you will have taken 30 steps towards your goal.

What are you willing to do in the next week to bring your vision into reality? Why one week? Because life happens one week, one day, one minute, one second at a time. In one week you can change the trajectory of your life. In one week you can realize a shift and chart measurable progress towards your goal.

Get into the habit of setting weekly Power Goals. The small changes will begin to shape your future. The vision that was once far away becomes closer—and you reinvent yourself one Power-filled week at a time.

Your Power Goals should be SMART; that's an acronym for Specific, Measurable, Achievable, Realistic, and Time-based. That way you can return to the plan and determine fairly quickly if the goals were accomplished. And *NO, you do not get to rest on Sunday*—instead, on that "day of rest," conduct a **15-minute** action towards accomplishing the week's goal.

Here's a sample One-Week Power Plan for Art. We will check in later to see what actions were taken within the week and what resulted from taking those actions.

Art's One-Week Power Plan

Three actions could move him toward his desired brand:

- **Goal 1:** Improve turnaround of project elements, installments, or revisions to no more than 48 hours.

- **Goal 2:** Send email follow-ups to all prospective Guru.com employers whose projects I have bid on but have not received a reply.

- **Goal 3:** Write holiday cards to send to all of my clients as a means of keeping in touch and establishing an ongoing rapport.

Here is Art's score for the week:

- **Goal 1:** I turned around two of my writing assignments within 48 hours, even over Thanksgiving Day. However, on a couple of others I exceeded the 48-hour turnaround time limit. This was partly due to my obligation to work holiday overtime hours at my retail job, which is not an excuse, but it was a factor.

- **Goal 2:** I sent follow-up notes to all five prospective Guru.com employers whose projects I have bid on; I received no replies, but the projects are still listed as "open" on the bid tracking page.

- **Goal 3:** My holiday cards are written out, signed, enveloped, stamped and ready to mail out later this week.

> ## COACH'S NOTE:
>
> How did you feel about your Power Goals? What results did you realize?

What I have learned from this Power Goals exercise— and indeed, from what Marva has been saying to me all along—is that *decisive and direct action* is necessary for success.

As part of this exercise, after only five follow-up letters to prospective Guru.com employers whose posted projects I had bid on, I have had a response from one who wants me to ghostwrite his book for him—and that was a posting that had expired. I could have written it off, and instead, the follow-up landed me the job!

Now, what more motivation for direct and decisive action could I possibly need? I believe I can say for a certainty that I am motivated enough to believe I can and will do better on my Power Plan for next week, and the week after that, and the week after that.

COACH'S NUDGE:

On the next page, write your Power Plan. Please take the challenge to change the trajectory of your life by writing your plan down. It starts with this one small step. Remember, these are measurable goals that you will accomplish within the course of a week and that are facets of your larger goal.

Reward success

If you are working with a partner or as a book club, hold a small celebration next week to acknowledge each person as they announce the **WOW** (Within One Week) accomplishments that I'm sure they will have!

Make copies of the next page, or create your own way to record and track your weekly Power Plan.

YOUR POWER PLAN Week of _____

LEADERSHIP

_____

_____

_____

What did you accomplish this week?

_____

_____

_____

_____

VISIBILITY

_____

_____

_____

_____

What did you accomplish this week?

_____

_____

_____

_____

CONSISTENCY

_____

_____

_____

What did you accomplish this week?

_____

_____

_____

_____

Do you think Larry Scott is the only soul brave enough to actually fulfill his dream and move to paradise? Or that Sue Thompson is the only person with enough discipline to change herself physically after age 50? Certainly, Art Lizza is not the only mid-career professional to muster the courage to change his career after age 50.

The following stories are written by three other people who I call EVERYDAY HEROES. Check out their inspiring stories. See if they don't inspire you!

What I Did For Love
The Quest of a Lifelong Learner

by Carla Dancy Smith

It is a myth that we learned all we need to know in Kindergarten—at least I did not. At age 50, I decided to return to school to complete a master's degree. I was already a successful consultant earning a respectable salary, but I had an undeniable urge to continue the acquisition of knowledge. I enjoy reading, writing, researching, intellectual debates, and experiential activities, so pursuing a master's degree was the next logical thing to do. Why not?

On May 11, 2008, at age 53, I listened to the Honorable Vernon Jordan deliver the American University Commencement address, anticipating my walk across the stage to receive my Master of Science degree in Organization Development (MSOD). I was seated strategically so that I could glimpse the smiling faces of my mother and father, both 70-years plus, who had traveled by train from Connecticut to be present. It was Mother's Day and what better gift could I give my parents, both of whom were obliged to forsake college to work and raise a family. Clapping loudly also were my two daughters, Camille and Celeste, 13 and 12 years old respectively. Later in the day, they shared with me their ideas and prospects for which universities they might attend to be "just like mom." They reminded me often that they deserved some credit and recognition on this occasion. It was true; they often accompanied me to the library to study and they helped me on several class projects.

Lovingly, I gazed upon Calvin, my husband of 15 years, who had picked up the slack and maintained the homefront during my many years of part-time collegiate life. He was a faithful proofreader of my school papers, and a reluctant guinea pig for me to test the theories and concepts I was digesting. Calvin often jokingly remarked that he was "attending sixth grade and eighth grade with my daughters and graduate school with my wife—all simultaneously, without the rewards."

My cousin from New Jersey, Michele Amad, a 2006 graduate of Rutgers University, was the official "seat saver" and photographer on this special day. The graduation ceremony was long, and it allowed ample time for me to reflect on both the glory in my story as well as the bumps, twists, roadblocks, detours, and near fatal occurrences over the past three years. It is only fair that I share the full picture of how I earned my robe and tassel on this day.

In retrospect, I wish someone had offered me "the inside scoop" or a "back to school cheat sheet" as I embarked on this learning quest, but no "guide-book" was available. First, I must confess that I've been down this road before. I was just nine hours short of a Master of International Communication from American University, class of 1993. But my education gave way to love, dating, engagement, marriage, and then children. The graduate credit hours lapsed, the degree requirements changed, the communication market shifted, and my interest abated, although only temporarily, but as it turned out, this was fortunate.

There is something about defeat that invigorates me to try even harder when given a second chance. This time my approach to graduate studies was methodical, intentional, and full of determination. In the months prior to my 50th birthday, I spent hours thinking and praying about what I wanted to do in the second half of my life. I am adept at reinventing myself, having already held many unrelated positions of ever-increasing responsibility in corporate America, always parlaying my old skills and gaining new ones to move to the next level. I now wanted to have the credentials to add credibility in the marketplace to certify my capabilities and worth.

My motivation for returning to school was selfish. I knew I needed to "keep it fresh" and update my professional toolkit in order to compete with all the smart Generation X and Y folks now in the workplace. Finances for school were not an obstacle because I was willing and able to secure needed student loans ($40K as it turned out). My desire to learn did not depend upon what others thought, what the immediate return on investment would be, or how hard the endeavor itself would be. I had an unfulfilled, lifelong-learner's dream and a deep desire to attain a master's degree. This was just as important to me as the lifestyle and income that I had achieved, and naturally wanted to maintain.

Over the course of a few months, I visited several local graduate school open houses, evaluated the program options, and weighed the pros and cons of traditional night classes versus a weekend, cohort program. I selected the latter because it was easier for me to plan and block the time on my calendars, both at home and at work. That program was also designed to be more "user-friendly" for the mature working professional—no GRE or GMAT entrance tests required. Executive programs value work experiences, as working professionals are the norm. The hardest part of the admissions process was writing the personal statement explaining why this course of study and degree pursuit was important to me. Passion, energy, and commitment in my heart were my personal selling points. I had to "begin with the end in mind" and with the unwavering resolve not to give up, no matter what.

I started graduate school in June 2005, with Cohort 52, at American University/National Training Laboratories. The class began with 12 fellow cohort members, ranging in age from 24 to 55. I was not the oldest class member, but I was the only person married with young children. I realized at the onset of our course work that it took me twice as long to write a paper or complete an assignment as some of my younger cohort members. I attributed it to rusty brain cells; on the bright side, I believed the research and the intense intellectual rigor would help fend off any onset of Alzheimer's disease. This was nothing new really, as I have always had to try harder to prove myself equally competent to others in the room—I was just a little older and wiser now.

All of my friends and professional colleagues share stories about our constant struggles to "do it all," to balance work and personal life. When I initially considered adding school to the mix of an already action-packed agenda, I knew it would be a challenge, but I could not have anticipated the breadth and depth of the mental and physical pain I was choosing to embrace as a "wannabe" graduate student. I was already wearing many hats— wife, mother, stepmom, daughter, daughter-in-law, friend...how hard could it be to add one more? Admittedly, I underestimated the answer to this question.

Fortunately, my employer, a large management consulting firm, is supportive of advanced education and offers generous tuition reimbursement, as well as flexible work schedules, to accommodate external training and education. However, I also had to temporarily remove myself from the consultant fast-track at the company. I was able to meet my client demands and billable hour targets, but I had to forego many extra-curricular networking and career enhancing opportunities. I could

not work late or accept demanding tight-deadline assignments, such as writing proposals. I declined partner-
driven special projects and highly visible tasks if they
were unpredictable in scope. I elected to assume an "under the radar" profile for the three years I was in graduate school. At the end of the journey I emerged as a
better consultant, but there were professional sacrifices
along the way.

At home, I became comfortable with a less than "hospital clean" house, piles of unopened mail, doing less
entertaining, and more dining on fast-food meals in the
evenings because I did not have the time to devote to my
usual duties. Yes, I felt guilty and overwhelmed. I developed an unhealthy routine of only four to five hours of
sleep nightly, so I could study after everyone went to
bed. I had an addiction to daily *venti* Starbucks in order
to cope and keep the adrenaline flowing. My personal
needs were ignored; I did not have time for exercise or
friends. I prayed a lot and I know that it was the grace of
God and my faith in His Son, Jesus Christ, that brought
me over the graduate school mountain.

I missed some important occasions, such as gradua-
tions, baby christenings, weddings, and other celebra-
tions due to the demands of school. I used every favor
and chit anyone in my support group would allow, as I
needed a lot of help to stay the course. I nicknamed these
dedicated family and friends "my tail wind." They were
all with me in spirit as I sat in the American University
auditorium on graduation day. I know I could not have
made the journey without them.

I am proud to be a lifelong learner and I invite you to
join me in feeding the mind and soul with the ceaseless
pursuit of knowledge. A master's degree is only one
marker of achievement, only one form of recognition.
There are so many other valuable opportunities for learning that carry their own significant rewards, both tangi-
ble and intangible.

As a mature student, there is an added feeling of accomplishment and satisfaction in gaining new skills and competencies. I would not mind if history remembers me in the same way that Grandma Moses is remembered—as a role model who successfully started a career in the arts at an advanced age and flourished. I am already secretly thinking about when I can start my PhD studies.

"Dr. Carla Dancy Smith" is possible, and so is your educational dream—whatever it may be. Go for it—and be willing to sacrifice to achieve your goal!

COACH'S TIP:

Educational information is readily available online, in libraries, community colleges, seminars, webinars, professional associations, and even through employers and peers.

Learning can take place anyplace and anytime these days, virtually and independently as well as in traditional classroom programs.

Fifty and <u>Fabulous</u>, Darling...
Choosing and Meeting the Challenge of a Lifetime

by Satori Shakoor

The first Saturday in June 2004, the air smells early morning fresh and the bright shining sun is a sharp contrast to my glum mood. My 50th birthday is five months away and what do I have to show for it? I fire up the car and wait for the metal parking lot gate to open. At 50 I should be a master at something. I'm on the way to the gym, my sanctuary of iron and sweat. My five-day-a-week workout has kept me sane, balanced, and lean for 25 years. This morning, however, I am neither balanced nor lean. I'm dissatisfied with the twenty-two plus pounds of extra fat that hides the proof of my five-day-a week routine. *Don't worry girl that lean and muscular body you've always had is underneath.* I am not consoled. "Underneath" is the operative word. It's underneath. I'm underneath. I'm hiding the mastery. The traffic light turns green as I guide my car down the ramp onto Detroit's John C. Lodge Expressway. *A bodybuilding contest... Yes! I'll do a bodybuilding contest to cele-*

165

brate my 50th birthday! The thought hits me like a ton of wonder as I accelerate and merge into traffic. I laugh out loud. It's perfect! Without a clue as to the enormity of the challenge or how profound the discoveries will be, I embark.

Soon I discover my relationship to the gym, working out, and my life. Over the years, going to the gym and working out has deteriorated into a mindless habit, much like my life. I'm bored, uninspired, and driven mostly by anxiety and fear. I'm afraid that if I miss a day, the fat monster will creep up and devour me in pounds and pounds of Haagen-Daz Butter Pecan misery and guilt. The idea of competing in a bodybuilding contest gives me a new way to think about the gym, my workouts, and my life. I'm excited. I want to know what's underneath the layers. What's possible if I go the extra mile into the realm of excellence? Training and excellence are added to my vocabulary. They become my approach to this higher purpose. No more workouts; I'm in training for my 50s.

My weakest muscle is my relationship to food. I need discipline and perhaps a small miracle when it comes to certain foods. I love Haagen-Dazs Butter Pecan ice cream, Snickers Bars and Lay's Barbecue Potato Chips. Oprah calls it "comfort food" and "emotional eating," but I call it, "just can't eat one." Fifty *is* emotional, damn it! Suddenly I'm hit with another thought. I've been substituting food for faith. I lack faith. Whoa! Until that moment, faith had been an unexamined frontier. Faith lived in my mind as a vague concept, an airy-fairy superstition at best. Things worked out because I was lucky, crossed my fingers, wished, hoped, prayed, and bargained with God. Food helped me endure the uncertainty while I waited and wondered if my hope would turn out. What I feared was the other side of faith, the devastating disappointment when things didn't turn out as I had hoped.

166

Being no stranger to disappointment, I know that it is very expensive. Disappointment costs time, money, and forward movement. The desire to bail out often, but not always, follows and that brings even more disappointment. The bodybuilding contest comes with a deadline; it's five months and one week before my 50th birthday. With no time to waste, I must move forward with discipline and faith. I struggle with discipline around food, moving forward with a clean diet, then backward with undisciplined eating. Back and forth, back and forth, no net gain.

Discipline and faith become practices that move me forward. Discipline gets me to the gym and on the treadmill by 7:00 a.m. Faith is in the application of three sets of fifteen focused reps for each muscle group in my body. Discipline is in the six small clean meals I eat each day. Faith is the investment in my personal trainer. He won't allow me to wallow in disappointments, setbacks, or beat myself up and waste time with a "poor me" attitude. My excitement leads me to join a community of bodybuilding folks; I learn more than anyone needs to know about diet, weight training, nutrition, vitamins, supplements and yes, discipline.

Discipline becomes a form of love. Love points me to my future. Discipline is in the steps I take to get there and faith is the guarantee that I will arrive. This way to success, that way to setback and failure, the choice is mine every single day. Faith travels light. Criticism and judgment is extra baggage. Faith allows me to take only the lessons from my choices. Discipline encourages me to make the more powerful choice.

After the first month, the weight loss is evident and I'm encouraged. The second month I'm bursting with energy. I can see the fat melt away to reveal the muscle cuts. Highly motivated, I chant a new mantra, "No fat between me and God." I feel like a sculptor and my body is the marble. Burning fat, building muscle, and being

167

very disciplined around diet and exercise are my chiseling tools. To neglect any one of these areas is to be out of sync with my goal and intention. By month three, I'm a machine. Foods outside of my committed goal are no longer relevant. I feel great! People stop and ask, "Are you a dancer?" "How did you get your arms like that?" Strangers want to touch my biceps and my niece wants to be like me when she grows up. Only 10% of people go where I am going. I become an anonymous spokeswoman for health and fitness in the circles I travel.

My trainer and I attend a few bodybuilding contests to see what they're like and what to expect. It's a different world that has its own unique rules, regulations, and smells that permeate the auditorium or theatre: boiled eggs, un-bathed tanned bodies wearing bronzers, chocolate, Pam cooking spray and other oils to show the body to best effect under the lights. It's a world of competing bodies, where the healthiest, muscular, most symmetrical and graceful are crowned king and queen. The parade of the top 10% of bodies is breathtaking. The posing suits are spectacular and the contest is entertaining.

After observing all the categories, I decide to compete in the figure category. This is a contest of symmetry, grace, and beauty. In the figure category, women present their sculpted bodies in a one-piece and two-piece posing suit. They perform four quarter-turn poses for a panel of judges while wearing three-to-six-inch clear heel platform shoes. Yes, the "pole-dancer" kind of clear heels that Chris Rock wants to keep his daughters away from.

By month five, two weeks before the contest, I'm 10% body fat, 90% muscle; my body is beautiful, starving, and ready to pose in the contest. I have two beautiful posing suits made and purchase a pair of the requisite clear heel shoes. Learning to walk in them proves to be the hardest part. A six-foot-four drag queen offers to teach me to walk with grace. I look 25, have the wisdom of half a century, and can walk like a runway model on the clear heel stilts.

On the day of the contest, I'm dizzy, excited, and starving. My trainer and my sister are backstage to give support—along with friends who are in the audience. I feel a bond with the other women who are competing. Each has her own story of how she got there. I realize I was never in competition with these women, only myself. Finally it's my turn to pose. I make the quarter-turn poses like a champ in those heels. It takes five minutes. Five minutes after all those months of work! I win second place in the figure category. I lose by one point to a woman 15 years my junior. Afterwards, I overhear people comment "She (meaning me) was robbed." If they only knew! I smile at the compliment and run my hand over the encasement of the Samurai sword I have won and marvel at the engraved title, "2004 NANBF (North America Natural Bodybuilding Federation) Annual Michigan Open, Figure Short Division, Second Place." Robbed? I don't think so. The contest was won five months ago on that bright sunny day when I decided to compete. It was won when I nurtured faith and chose excellence to usher in my 50th year. I had become Queen Midas; confident that anything I touched and invested in, would turn to gold.

Most importantly, I learn that faith is a vision of a future that begins with a self firmly rooted in now.

Faith is maintained by keeping the vision of that future alive and always in sight.

Faith is a practice maintained by actions taken, big and small, toward a goal that at times seems impossible and surely unreachable. Faith is compassion; it does not shout or scold my weaknesses. Faith seeks only to strengthen them, that I may reach my intended goal. Faith is impossible to lose, but always vulnerable to be misplaced.

169

Faith must be practiced and, when practiced, faith offers the opportunity to get back on track.

If I pick up a pound or two or ten, I don't fear the fat monster anymore. The fat monster has been mastered and swallowed up by my future. From here I can look back see the bridge that faith and discipline have built and map the wonders of every step taken.

The future has a fabulous view darling. No wonder they call it "The Fabulous Fifties!"

My Reinvention Process
A Day of Reckoning

by Alford Day

It was a day I will never forget, March 31, 2000. I went through my normal business day routine. I woke up in the morning, said my prayers, got my daughters off to school, and headed out to work.

Each morning as I step off the elevator, before entering my office, I always say a prayer asking God to help me handle any business matters that I might confront. Little did I know that this day would change my business and personal life forever.

Prior to this day, my multimillion-dollar healthcare businesses were flourishing. Revenues and profits were up; new employees were being hired on a regular basis. We had just won a couple of new large government contracts. I had even opened up offices in Africa.

Then I received a phone call from my favorite government client. I was actually kind of excited to hear from this client because this was the last day of a three-year contract, a contract that the firm had performed very well on and now it was time to get paid. The call went like this: "Hey, Alford, I got some good news and bad news...the good news is that your firm did an out-

171

standing job on the contract and we are going to give you an outstanding past performance review—but the bad news is that your $300,000 outstanding close-out invoice will not be paid until three years from today."

I anxiously said, "Not be paid? What do you mean? We have already performed the services and you just stated we did an outstanding job."

However, there was a technical problem that only time would resolve. He proceeded to say he had reviewed the malpractice insurance policy on the doctors we hired over the past year. The insurance firm never added the rider to the policy that would absolve the government from being sued for any possible malpractice issues that may arise, for up to three years after the last day of the contract.

I vehemently stated that I knew we had purchased the insurance rider and he must be mistaken. That's when he said he'd talked with my human resources people numerous times over the past several months, reminding them to please buy the additional coverage, to no avail.

I immediately marched down to my human resources department and questioned the guy who was in charge of this matter. He looked me in the eye and was clearly in great pain as he said he was "sorry." He said he was just overwhelmed with his work and forgot to do it.

That meant I would not be paid that $300,000 until three years later, on March 31, 2003. As a business owner, you make mistakes over a period of time, but this mistake was catastrophic to the cash flow. The firm would never recover.

With the assurance of a $300,000 accounts receivable payment arriving in 60 days, from the government no less, I had already borrowed against that money for payroll and other related expenditures. Needless to say, cash flow would now become a major problem. Moreover, I knew my bank was going to hit the roof when they learned of this. How would the firm survive during this disaster of Katrina proportions?

In a couple of months I would turn 50. My business was about to begin its three-year death march into oblivion. As I began to figure out how to fight off my financial alligators, I took a Landmark Education class. This was an awesome self-help class. I was able to search into my childhood to get a sense of the personal hang-ups, which might have become communication and growth blocks for me now, as an adult. Fortunately, I was able to identify and put to rest some personal issues, which would turn out to help me get through the turbulent upcoming years. My 50th birthday was a great day and despite everything, I felt very positive about the upcoming decade.

I was familiar with the process of reinventing myself. I spent considerable time reinventing myself during my 20s. In college, I was a pre-med student and would later spend a couple of years in dental school, only to drop out. That was pretty devastating for me. I was 25 years old, living in Boston, some 800 miles away from my Detroit home, with no money and no job. I did not want to return home. I would struggle for years to find my next goal, but through prayer and God's grace I was able to get there. I went back to school, got my Master of Public Health from Boston University and relocated to Washington, D.C.

Eventually I rebuilt my business. However, my firm was never able to recover from that unpaid $300,000 invoice. My business life became a real bear.

I was able to keep the company afloat for a long time because I did have a rainy day account set aside that enabled me to make payroll and pay expenses. And we secured several additional contracts.

However, my bank eventually closed my account and a couple of years of constantly robbing Peter to pay Paul finally caught up with me. I could no longer hold back the hurricane.

The financial floods, coupled with employee defections and client dissatisfaction, led me to file for Chapter 11 bankruptcy. I would ultimately lose millions of dollars in savings and future contract earnings. I subsequently got a divorce and even became ill for a while. Additionally, because of poor legal advice regarding my bankruptcy, I have a major lawsuit pending against those lawyers. The final chapter is yet to be told, but one thing was for sure, when my business failed, another reinvention was about to get under way.

Despite my 20s reinventing experiences, reinventing myself in my 50s has been extremely difficult. You would think that because I had done it before, I would have a sense of perspective that would make this reinvention process easier. When you are young you feel that no matter what happens there is always plenty of time to recover. It's like buying life insurance at a young age when you think you are going to live forever. When you hit 50, you suddenly realize that you are fast approaching the autumn of your life. You realize you're not going to live forever. Many of your friends and family have died and you're fast approaching retirement age.

You now spend more time looking back over your life and reassessing your past decisions than you spend focusing on what your future might look like. When you were young, you were fearless about your future. Now, depending on how your life turned out, the fear of looking forward can be extremely painful. Getting that AARP card in the mail can be another jarring moment. You think, wow! Am I really a senior citizen?

As an entrepreneur for 25 years, I had grown accustomed to living at a certain financial level. That lifestyle has come to a sudden halt. Financial sustainability is now the goal—this as a divorced, single dad, taking care of my 90-year-old mother.

Prayer and faith in God were the cornerstone principles that enabled me to survive my early years. These principles were instilled in me by my parents and they would be the principles that would guide me into the next important phase of my life.

My reinvention process started out with an evaluation of my life's failures and success, as well as determining my actual skill set.

Here's how I went about the process: I spent months writing my skills down, and I solicited friends, family members, and other business cohorts to provide some commentary to this process. I prayed daily, read biblical scriptures and meditated quietly, in secret places. From reading the scriptures I was able to get a better understanding of the term "God's will" and what that might look like in my life.

For the majority of my life I made most career choices based on what I wanted to do, rather than seeking to understand if this choice was "God's will" for me. Yes, God allows us to make our own choices in life, but when you choose to live in "His will," your life will be a lot less complicated. Now I understand that. So I decided that whatever I was going to do, this time I wanted to live according to "His will."

After reviewing my past experiences and evaluating the comments of those in my circle of influence, I decided my most important attributes and skills are these: spirituality, speaker, entrepreneur, educator, motivator, leader, administrator, visionary, and giver. The question I wrestled with for almost a year was in what context would I use this skill set to live according to what God wants for me?

- Do I look for a job at my age?

- Should I start another business, maybe a not-for profit organization?

- Should I go to divinity school, get remarried, or devote all of my time to my kids and ailing mother?

After many months of prayer and meditation, I was led to an understanding that an entrepreneurship ministry would be the foundation through which God would manifest my best life. My skill set would now be used as a blessing for others.

From this revelation, I was led to write a book on business; become a motivational speaker and business coach; volunteer my time with the Small Business Administration to help others start businesses; work with a church prison ministry to help departing prisoners start businesses; and start my own business radio show on the Internet.

In summary, I have now chosen to live within God's design for my life, thus making my transformation (this time) less arduous than that of my youth, as well as more fulfilling.

Coach's Commentary

Did these three stories spark any ideas?

After reading the testimony of these three everyday heroes, I hope you see there are no excuses to prevent you from reaching your own reinvention goals.

We must live this life with urgency and purpose. At this age, the one thing that we should ALL know for sure is that tomorrow is not promised. So, what are you waiting for? What excuses are you making for not living your life, NOW?

Fifty, **50, half a century, half of a dollar, 50%, half full, halfway...**

Lots of people are living to 100 years old and beyond, so the idea that it is too late to address the things you want in life is ludicrous, ridiculous, preposterous, and even *nonsensical.* "Heavens to Murgatroid!" *(Ah... excuse the baby boomer's Saturday cartoon flashback!).*

NOW is exactly the right time to take a leap of faith and pursue your dreams. **Wake up to life.**

Got a pocket full of lemons? Make lemonade.

Rocked by unexpected circumstances? See opportunity in the waves, instead of crisis on the seas.

Feeling afraid? Acknowledge the fear and then do it anyway!

But, first gird yourself with preparation: **do the work**, create the strategy, line up your resources and follow the undone in your life. Fifty isn't the end—it's the beginning of a quest to get better, stronger and wiser.

If you've always wanted to go to school—**GO!**

If you want to learn how to sky dive—**DO IT!**

If you want 6-pack, 3-pack, or just no-flab abs—**GET BUSY!**

If you want to write a book, change your look, start a new career or take up a new hobby…take a leap of faith and get started.

Honestly…if not now, WHEN?

...But Not the End

December 5, 2008

There's a party over here!

I hear and feel the familiar thud of the plane doors closing, and the plane shudders into motion. I am on my way to Detroit for my 50th birthday party.

My sister Marcia and my cousins Sheryl, Bernadine, and Preston are hosting friends and family to help me usher in my decade of new beginnings.

We roll toward the runway, and I begin to say a little prayer as we prepare for take-off.

My prayer is one of gratitude. I give thanks for all of the many blessings that God has given me: good health, loving family and friends, the health of my family and friends, a bountiful income, a home, an open heart, an active mind, an enlightened spirit, and all of the blessings that I have yet to receive.

And to that prayer I add my gratitude for the role YOU have played in my journey. I am grateful to you for bringing my vision of NOW into a reality.

Peace and blessings,

Marva

179

ADDENDUM

Don't be scared! Make social media your new best friend

When this book was first written, I had only just begun to utilize social marketing as a tool. The tool has been so fantastic, I had to write this addendum to share what I have learned with you.

In the 21st century we are seeing the most amazing technological, information, and social revolution ever with Web 2.0 social media (interactive online communication), including Internet marketing opportunities available for everyone to optimize. Incredibly, social networking options are free at the entry-level, making them excellent and cost-effective marketing tools for job search and business marketing strategies. Social media is not limited to young folks, but enables everyone to facilitate communication with live human beings across space and time zones.

That's why if you're actively engaged in a branding effort in search of a new job or to expand business leads, you'll need to learn, join and use social networking opportunities—to continually reinvent and freshen up your brand image and expertise in the face of fluctuating economic and social conditions.

Occasionally, I have asked friends "Are you on Facebook?" They look at me the way some people look at older women in mini-skirts and *too* much makeup and say, "No. My kids are." If you are reading this book, chances are likely that your age is in the vicinity of 50. If you think Facebook and Twitter are only for your kids... please reassess your position.

If it seems like an overwhelming proposition, take baby steps:

- **Use social networking to keep in touch with friends and family first.** I am now in touch with people that I have not seen, talked to and in some cases even thought about in 30 years. It has been wonderful to just check in with them, occasionally comment on something they have posted, or provide an unexpected lead or share information from which they might benefit.

- **Develop a visible and credible online profile to create social media that will enhance your online-branding effort.** Some sites are more personal than business, but always be aware of the image projected by the photos you post (or are posted by others).

- **If you're a job-seeker or business owner, branding and expanding your online image and presence is an essential component for effective networking.**

- **Understand that if you are going in to business and you do not have an online presence, the absence of information is also a part of your brand**...the lack of data is then your brand instead.

After gaining confidence in these areas, you'll ask yourself (like I did); "Why didn't I join social sites like Facebook, LinkedIn, and Twitter (I'm still working on this one) sooner?"

The twin goals of this section are to show you how easy it is:

- To get familiar with social networking

- To put into practice your own social networking strategy—for free. What have you got to lose?

Let me share my story. I signed up with LinkedIn (the leading social site for professional and business people) in December 2004 purely to stop friends from bugging me about joining. You've probably received some of these emails, too. I joined, and it took me two years to understand the importance of creating a credible profile. Over the next two years I would build my network to 177 connections. Collectively, these 177 connections have over 56,800 connections. LinkedIn allows you access to the third level of business connections. In my case, I now have access to over 4 million people (by introduction from the first and second level of connections). I have not even begun to use this feature.

I recognize these vast numbers as potential—people with different ideas, different experiences and untapped genius. Soon after joining, I purchased a book called, *"You're on LinkedIn, Now What?"* I realized that I should try to understand how to optimize the power of this network. I read one chapter at a time, and did exactly what the author suggested. The chapter called *Groups* was of particular interest to me because I have always believed in the "power of group genius" and the ability to expand one's reach and breadth by engaging others in your work. I joined 30 affinity groups.

The first set of groups that I joined were for organizations that I belong to such as Michigan State University and Harvard Kennedy School alumni, Crain's 40 Under 40...you get the picture. Then I joined issue-related groups: human resources, baby boomer, training and consulting.

Here are a few examples of how I worked with my new best friends:

As I mention in Chapter 6, part of my branding strategy is to become more visible to human resource professionals. In June 2009, the Society of Human Resource Management (SHRM) selected me to present on the first day of this prestigious annual conference. My time slot was at 7:00 a.m. Of course, I was concerned about whether anyone would actually show up. I posted a question on LinkedIn to my human resources groups (over 10,000 people).

This is my first time speaking at the National SHRM Conference (Monday, June 28 at 7:00 AM). The topic is personal branding. Do you plan to attend the conference?

Any suggestions? Please join me.

My plea for company received responses with suggestions from about 20 people; and a handful of people promised to attend my "early riser" session on Personal Branding. I do not know how many people read the question, or how many showed up as a result of this invitation, but I had made my first foray into tapping the power of the LinkedIn group function.

After publishing my book, *Branding Yourself After Age 50: Creating Brand Strategy for Life*, to celebrate my rite of passage when I turned 50 in December 2008, I posed a question to the baby boomer group members (about 1,000 people):

> I recently published a book titled, *Branding Yourself After Age 50*. Other than AARP, do you have any suggestions for conferences/venues where I can speak about personal branding and/or sell my books? Thank you.

The floodgates opened to reveal amazing leads—as if I'd struck oil. From this question, I received about 35 responses ranging from suggestions on associations and websites to people I should contact. Most impressively, one response led to a radio interview in Sacramento, California (Living Well Radio NewsTalk 1530 KFBK) and another led to conducting two webinars for Georgetown University alumni. In addition, I was invited to present a workshop for a 50+ networking group in Michigan, which would provide me with my first book signing event. I felt like a star! The amazing thing is that these leads and opportunities were **all from people who had never laid their eyes on me**—with the exception of my profile picture.

It should be obvious now why I had to write this section to share the good news about social networking. It is a must—especially for the 50 and over crowd. You will not be alone. Learn how to tap into **the power of unlimited group genius.**

There is also the other side of the coin, which is *answering* questions. When you begin to share your expertise with others, you are branding yourself online as an expert in your field. But make sure that the information provided is correct! I look for opportunities to provide the same exceptional experience to others that I continue to enjoy with my new best friends.

So, what is "Web 2.0" social media?

The most astounding invention of the 21st century is undoubtedly Web 2.0 social media. Why? Web 2.0 allows everyone free platforms to build their own weblogs. Web 1.0 accesses information from traditional websites built at great cost by web designers and programmers. With DIY (do-it-yourself) interactive Web 2.0, however, YOU write and control your own weblog (as the term indicates, it's a contraction of website and blog), updating and spinning info without having to learn computer code, or hire an expensive programmer. Web 2.0 enables easy interaction with people from across the globe.

Do you see why DIY Web 2.0 social media is a communication revolution that's also social in promoting contact based on an ever-growing foundation of trustworthy friends? You are in complete control of what you want to share with them and the whole wide world (www.)—through your own weblog!

Benefits to Job Seekers:

- Posting a professional profile of your experiences, names of contacts for references, volunteer projects, awards and other pertinent info on your blog for easy access.

- Posting a video resume for prospective employers "to meet" you on YouTube. Type in "video resume" to see what other job seekers are doing.

Benefits to Business Owners:

- Posting a company profile with a description of services and related info on your weblog.

- Posting info-filled blogs (also known as articles) at least twice weekly as lead-ins to your website.

- Ongoing opportunities to target thousands and possibly millions of sales leads!

Why is social media so effective?

- Especially in an age of "social disconnect," it's an engaging way to feel connected and to find new friends; or reacquaint yourself with old friends.

- Your "friends" are already pre-selected by the nature of the social sites you join.

- You enjoy the convenience of just a few clicks that allow you to reach employers and prospects, which saves time and money—not to mention going green and saving resources.

- Best of all, membership is free at the entry-level. The sites are self-sustaining with add-ons and higher levels of membership for purchase if you so wish.

Whether you're on a mission to hunt down a good-fit job regardless of the economy or seeking to expand your business by generating free leads, you've got to learn the true value of grasping and applying DIY social media. Begin by blogging.

Go to www.youtube.com and type in, "How do I create a blog?" Or, go to www.wordpress.org for easy, how-to steps to download their free software to get started.

As I write this chapter, I'm segueing into webinars— new interactive online workshops that are a variation of social networking for professional training. Hosted by Maestro Conference, http://maestroconference.com, these webinars are very different from traditional tele-seminars. Participants break up into smaller groups, interact with and learn from each other, and return to main seminar sessions—all from Internet convenience.

I plan to host a series of these webinars each month. Participants will be given an opportunity to meet like-minded individuals, share ideas, and network in a dynamic environment that combines the convenience of traditional conference calls with the **interactivity of a live workshop**. The only thing missing is the parking fee and the ability to see and touch your neighbor. However, if a connection is made during the webinar series, participants may exchange contact information.

What about Twitter?

You may have heard of Twitter, the microblogging service logging only 140 characters for each post. Well, it's a great way to learn effective and efficient editing while communicating clearly. My friend Karen Batchelor, a life coach and Internet marketer, has her own website about Twitter at www.tweetlifeblog.com. Her story is an amazing one.

"I went from ground zero to having 5,633 Twitter followers in six months," Karen told me. It helps that Karen's a member of multiple social-sites. "Facebook laid the foundation for me. From there I joined LinkedIn and then Twitter," she said.

Karen's tips to Twitter success

Twitter is a great tool to brand your unique capabilities and experiences, with the potential to keep growing "followers" eager to learn from you. Here are Karen's tips to imprint a knock-out Twitter brand.

- Keep your posts helpful and useful. That's how you make friends and followers eager to learn from you—info that's entertaining and inspirational.

- As soon as you sign on, immediately post an engaging bio—in 160 characters.

- Highlight your first three points as a professional, and end the last point on a personal note, preferably humorous. Karen's bio is "Lawyer, former corporate exec now certified coach BIG into helping you achieve a transformational career or midlife makeover."

- Experiment with and create an online color brand. Go to a fabric store and drape different-colored fabrics for a backdrop to see which color best reflects your personality. Use this color to develop your online brand. (Karen's is a rich, vibrant red, as you can see.)

- Use a flattering current photo.

- Instead of using a stock Twitter background, which immediately announces you're a newbie, customize one that's different and unique to you.

- Pick a user name you're comfortable with, something like a pen name.

- For your background info, give three items—favorite books, movies, etc.

- As an analogy, Karen says she'd rather not have company if her house is not yet looking its best—so, in the same manner, prepare and create your Twitter brand before signing on.

That's all it takes to get started—some planning and getting over your hesitation. Karen likes to quote Emily Dickinson's, "Dwell in possibility."

I hope this section has been helpful to you. There are so many resources available on the web. Don't overlook this important tool in your networking toolkit. Get over your reticence quickly. If you haven't joined a social site yet, you're missing out on a global, social revolution that's unlike any. By quantum leaps and bounds you can expand your knowledge and possibly your career and business success.

Good luck with your efforts!

Appendix

Survey Questions

I conducted a survey of 100 persons over the age of 49. Here's what they said about turning 50—and living their 6th decade.

NOW THAT YOU ARE 50, WHAT DO YOU KNOW FOR SURE?

- Change is a beautiful thing.

- That I don't know anything for sure, and the best part is I don't <u>have</u> to know anything for sure.

- That life is to be celebrated and regrets are a waste of time; learn the lesson and keep moving.

- I know for sure that I still feel the same way inside as I did when I was ten years old, wondering what I will be when I "grow up."

- The happiest people are in careers they enjoy.

- God wants me to love <u>me</u> more, and consequently love others more too.

- That life is meant to be enjoyed and the 'little stuff' isn't worth destroying relationships over.

- I still love my wife on the good days, and like her on bad days.

- No more buts…You do not have to know exactly what you want to do, or where you want to go, at all times.
- You can follow a lead and pursue a dream, as long as you have the energy to do it.
- There is no one right way to do things and you can be successful figuring out your own way.
- I don't have to be threatened by others who are successful—I can learn from them without feeling like a child. Instead, I'm an equal, with an inquisitive nature, seeking all the wisdom I can gather.
- Need to enjoy life more; fifty is not an impending doom, it is just another phase of life.
- I'm 65 and I know I'll never go backwards. And I like the scenery from here.
- I still have a lot to offer the world!
- Life just keeps getting better, but one can't take it for granted. We must take care of the one body we have.
- A spiritual life, along with family and friends, is essential to finding meaning in life.
- Fifty is not old, but as we age, it takes a little more time, money and effort to stay healthy and youthful.
- I know perhaps even less than I knew (or thought I knew) before. I might be more willing to allow complexity and difficulties to assert themselves, as opposed to trying to simplify and "manage" things.
- Life is too short.
- With age comes wisdom.
- I probably will have to continue working for at least 15 more years.
- Trust but verify. Work before play. Faith is a gift to receive, not a goal to achieve. Learn forever.
- A good part of success is one's mental state (attitude). I'm beyond the halfway mark.
- At 55, I know that I will need to be more health conscience than I have ever been in the past.

- I now know that nothing is more important than family.
- I now know that nothing is worth losing my temper.
- I am 61 and I take a little more care of myself and not so much of others.
- I take vitamins every morning, walk, and I am a little more with God.
- I am settled and grounded. It's a nice feeling.
- I would take to heart the old Southern piece of wisdom: You wouldn't care what people thought of you if you knew how seldom they did.
- Nothing is for certain, or forever.
- Carpe Diem—seize the day!
- Older truly is wiser.
- I am getting old.
- Hot flashes are for real.
- Who my friends are that I can depend on.
- There is still a lot I don't know for sure.
- Sex is better!
- Taking care of my health is important.
- No one is perfect.
- I can do whatever I want to do and be happy!
- I need to get in better physical health.
- If you don't take care of yourself, it will really slow you down.
- "Willingness without action is fantasy." Take action; do not just fantasize.
- Love is always worth the effort. My life is full because of all the loved ones in it.
- I work hard to keep my mind sharp so I can remember every friend I have ever known.
- Life is too short to worry too much (but, of course, I do anyway).

- What other people think of you is unimportant. Be true to yourself.
- I know what I like and what I don't like—and I know what I want to do and what I don't want to do—and I'm not afraid to say "No!"
- I don't like parties. I like to write. I'm a loner who needs people. I know who I am. Exercise makes me feel good. I'm less vain every year.
- Life only gets better, your confidence level rises, and you really don't care what people think—but, I never did.
- I want to do all the things I've put off.
- I did not know anything when I was 30.
- I like me!
- I like to organize people, places and things.
- I enjoy being with family and friends.
- I no longer need to be a size 10 or 12 for that matter, but I do need to know my blood pressure and cholesterol numbers and be healthy.
- It's not as bad as I expected.
- Things always change.
- Love and affirmation are essential—in any form.
- Loss and pain are inevitable-suffering is optional.
- I know less than I did when I was 20!
- I made a number of mistakes in my career, in my 20s and 30s. However, they have all been great learning experiences.
- I am more confident in my 50s and having more fun.
- I'm a complete person with a great deal of room for continued growth.
- I don't have 50 more years left.
- It sure made all that heartache over turning 40 seem ridiculous.

- I do not know all the answers. In fact, I'm still working on the questions.
- Life really begins at 50.
- I am determined.
- I'm 63. I know that life and time are precious gifts and people, not things, really matter.
- I enjoy life.
- Life is about adjusting to change.
- Being almost 70 is not so bad.
- Life is short. Make the most of every day.
- I speak my mind with confidence. I've earned it.
- Relationships with family and friends are what are most important in life.
- I know that I'll never know everything I want to know.
- I wouldn't get married before turning 30, at least.
- I'm strong, yet fragile.
- My identity changes to grandmother!
- I still get excited and interested in many things going on around me.
- We all know what makes us happiest Go there and do not be distracted by the siren songs of pop culture or any other forms of pressure to conform.
- I don't want to be younger, but I wish my body was in better shape.
- The older I get, the less I know. I appreciate my "girl" friends.
- Life is so short, and I have more time behind me than I have in front of me.
- I know that turning 60 is just a finger snap away. I know that the only thing one can count on is change. I know that it is important to live each day to its fullest. I know that it is important to be silly.
- Don't waste time.

- Patience is truly a virtue.
- There is a living God that loves me in spite of me.
- Mirrors are everywhere. When I judge someone, or something, that is my projection. I'm using them or it to project something within me that I either admire or reject.
- I love myself.
- I like me—I'm OK.
- I have more self-confidence and I am more secure.
- I am surer of myself in an uncertain world.
- I have turned the corner.

IF YOU COULD DO ONE THING OVER AGAIN, WHAT WOULD IT BE?

- Absolutely nothing! I've loved my journey through good times and bad, so far...
- Abuse my body less.
- Enjoy everything I did more and stay in the moment.
- Nothing.
- Not be afraid to live.
- Watch my health.
- I think everything has gone as it should have. Sometimes I regret getting married right after high school and not going to college—but then I still have had a wonderful life.
- Research careers in my field better. I think I would have eventually worked in academia.
- I would have invested more money earlier.
- Spend more family time with my children when they were younger.
- Take more risks.
- Kiss butt.

- I would have set aside my fears and flown earlier.
- Prepare better financially.
- Get divorced sooner.
- Have more children.
- I would have married a different person than my ex.
- I would have stayed in college and earned a degree.
- Entered therapy earlier.
- Learned a lot more about childhood development before having kids. And appreciate them a lot more while I have them.
- Set educational goals and finish them.
- Less attention to the Men in My Life; they are important, but not as paramount as my mother told me they were.
- Kept playing cello.
- Get a master's degree.
- Get into a scientific field.
- Pull my son out of public school by the 2nd grade.
- Make better financial decisions.
- Stayed in real estate instead of quitting after the first 6 months, back in 1978.
- I would travel to Europe or to Alaska.
- Finish college.
- Can't think of anything that wouldn't have a ripple effect on things I wouldn't want to change. So I've accepted my faults and mistakes, tried to learn from them, and I'm looking ahead.
- Not marry.
- Stay in school and get an advanced degree before having a family and travel the world.
- Enjoy my teenage years.
- Say "No" more often and not be such a people pleaser.

- Dated more before marriage.
- Be a stricter parent.
- I would have embraced my twenties and early thirties instead of wishing I was older.
- I would have worn my bathing suit proudly instead of always covering up!!
- I would have been more aggressive (in a good way) in trying to make all my good ideas come to life. I backed off too much.
- I would have danced more.
- I would go to art school.
- My career choice—I would go directly into filmmaking instead of doing it in mid-career.
- I don't live with regrets—not worth the while!
- Not bail out of my marriage so fast; should have given it a better chance to survive.
- Nothing, I'm "just fine" can't go back, only forward.
- Marry better & later in life (Married at 17, had kids at 19).
- I suppose I would have gotten rid of my ex earlier and I would have taken more history in college and fewer courses from the lefty radicals—fun though they were.
- Pay attention in college! Meet and befriend those who do not look like me.
- Have sex a lot earlier and with a lot more men!
- Talk more frankly with my mother; she died almost a year ago.
- Spend time with Kevin in the cottage.
- Fulfill my aspirations to be an entrepreneur at an earlier age.
- I wish I had known myself better at an earlier age—like 21.
- Spend more quality, non-hassled time with my daughter.

- Enter marriage with more long-term thought and less emotion.
- Keep contact with everyone I have met in a much better way.
- Changed jobs 15 years ago....or gone in a different direction right out of college.
- Go to law school.
- Marry my 2nd husband first.
- I would have worked harder to have understood one of my sons when he was a teenager.
- Know more about the law and medicine.
- Be an artist.
- I would not have married at 19.
- I would have asked my ex-husband to leave several years before I finally did and created a much more fulfilling and less-stressed life for all of us sooner than I did.
- I'd redo the educational experience, beginning with college and continue toward a PhD.
- Realize how quickly your family grows up and stay more in the present.
- I was raising my children in the late sixties and seventies, the height of the feminist movement and its attendant insanities. I was stupid enough to respond by trying to prove my worth—a housewife had no worth in that world. It is not to say that the movement did not improve life for women, but back then feminism was strident and did not recognize what its mission should have included—a choice to not burn your bra.
- Not so much partying in my 20s.
- I wouldn't dress my four girls alike.
- Love more men and stay single.
- I would have started my candy business sooner.
- Marry my first love.

- Been a more understanding husband.

WHAT HAS BEEN THE MOST EXCITING CHANGE THAT YOU HAVE EXPERIENCED DURING THIS LAST HALF CENTURY?

- The change in consciousness in America that we just witnessed in the 2008 presidential campaign.
- Accepting myself.
- Realizing I care about myself more than I care about what people think of me.
- I've become what I always wanted to be.
- Finding that there is still time to make a positive difference in the world.
- Civil Rights Movement
- Realizing that I am in control and only I have power over my feelings.
- The knowledge of the world extending beyond home - other climates, cultures and geography.
- I now live alone. Finally I am all right with it. As a matter of fact, it's exciting to see what options are here for me at this age.
- Buying my company and watching it and my employees grow. And my second marriage to my true soul mate.
- Magellan, Garmin and GPS; Google Earth!
- A tremendous sense of freedom! I have always known myself to be a "late bloomer," and the time has come to bloom. I feel a deep confidence in my instincts and a willingness to hear correction that makes sense. I'm not afraid to try and not afraid to fail.
- Enjoying hobbies and personal interests more.
- More women in politics! And I keep trying to work to get more women elected so I get our half in my lifetime.

- Owning my own business.

- Traveling the world, seeing my children become successful on their own right, getting to know my granddaughters and spending time with them, seeing my mom grow old in good health and good spirits, sharing great times with friends and family, having a wonderful federal career and then a successful business, and creating wealth--all wonderful.

- Being an aunt, great aunt and grandparent. Children bring smiles, hugs, kisses, and squeals of love and affection that just make my heart sing.

- Personally, my personal growth. Globally, the Internet.

- The Internet—by far a life-altering method of communication has opened up my horizons beyond my little world.

- Becoming a grandmother and great-grandmother

- The freedom to live in the center of activity via the Internet.

- Virtual communication

- The end of the Cold War and its existential threat.

- Space exploration

- Being able to travel to places that I have never visited before (especially via cruises).

- I've fallen in love and gotten married, I've returned to the real estate field.

- The most exciting change in my life has been to move to the USA, a new culture. To live in a society with rights, and in a democracy.

- The transition into the computer and communication age.

- Opportunities for women are growing—not as quickly as we 60s feminists hoped—but enough to give us continued hope for our daughters and granddaughters.

- Liberation

- Gaining extensive knowledge about so many different things (personal and professional) and earning financial freedom.
- I am happily married.
- Not only knowing that I have freedoms, such as financial and emotional, but going with it.
- Understanding God's love and loving who I am.
- Starting a more active lifestyle.
- Education and travel
- Growing in my spiritually.
- Global awareness, computers
- Respect for women and people of other races and cultures have increased greatly.
- Medical technology
- Going from smart paper processing to very smart electronics.
- I'm thrilled to be living now and seeing this presidential election. When I was born, it would not have been imagined.
- Becoming myself.
- Enjoying life to the fullest.
- Wisdom and patience.
- Approaching greater racial, gender and religious equity.
- Growth and respect of women in all fields.
- I birthed two daughters. I birthed myself out of a bad marriage. I know I can birth myself again if I want. I have grandchildren who know and accept me more and more. I wrote a book and started an association. I maintain a great professional reputation, am a dutiful, beloved daughter, and part of a positive, loving relationship.
- Advent of the Internet.
- Owning my own business and becoming self directed.

- Divorce!
- Falling in true, true love.
- Becoming a mother.
- Getting married.
- Communication advances...Internet...cell phones
- I have loved watching my daughter grow up and now about to be married.
- Personally, maturing and liking myself more. Change in the world, the ease and speed of communication.
- Use of the computer.
- Better hair color.
- Being a grandmother.
- Technology...and I don't necessarily think it's been a wholly positive change.
- Giving birth and continuing to watch my children blossom. Carving new pathways in science that are making a difference.
- Obviously, technological advances, but I don't necessarily see all of them as positive. I HATE walking in the streets, riding the subways, etc., seeing everyone with their ears plugged up, missing the sounds of city, nature, not paying any attention to what's going on around them.
- Everyone is so self-absorbed, especially the youth.
- To see my kids grow up; to begin a new career; to feel strong, healthy, happy.
- Progress in medicine—I'm old enough to remember clearly what could kill you in the 50s and 60s. SO much progress in treatments and cures.
- Personally...raising children. Worldwide...the technology EXPLOSION.
- At 45, after my youngest left for college, I opened my own childcare center. This September, we celebrate our 25th anniversary—you can have it all, just not in the same year.

- Giving birth to my son, finishing a Ph.D., getting a contract for my first book, and rekindling my love for a former lover.

- Well, I think I have finally grown up. What a concept!

- The development of the African American middle class.

- I finally learned to have a balanced life between work, family and fun. I'm having more fun than at any age of my life. I am dancing—really!

- My self-assuredness; my love of experiencing the moment and being adventuresome.

THE AUTHORS

MARVA L. GOLDSMITH, a Certified Image Professional, helps clients create a road map and understand the role that image and personal branding—the packaging of talents and signature traits into a marketable image—play in their journey.

Marva knows the transformation process intimately because she has lived it. She began her career as an electrical engineer and later became a federal lobbyist and human resources strategist. Now, she uses her experience and diverse skill set to assist her clients with their professional transformation.

Marva studied image management with Dominique Isbecque International, the London Image Institute and the Image Resource Group. She has a Bachelor of Science degree from Michigan State University in Electrical Engineering and a Master's of Public Administration degree from Harvard University. She received additional leadership training through the Center for Creative Leadership and Georgetown University's Leadership Coaching Program.

CARLA DANCY SMITH is a "change coach." She partners with individuals and offers tools and techniques to help them change directions during milestone events. She offers workshops to teens rising from middle school to high school, and to students graduating from high school and progressing to college. She coaches individuals making a transition from one employment to a new endeavor or retirement.

Carla teaches diversity courses as an adjunct instructor and is a qualified Myers-Briggs Type Indicator (MBTI) assessment administrator. She has a Master's of Science degree in Organization Development (MSOD) from the American University/ National Training Laboratory (AU/NTL) located in Washington, DC; and a Bachelor of Science: Business Administration, from Rockhurst Jesuit College in Kansas City, Missouri. Carla has written and published articles, given speeches, and is a member of many professional organizations—and prides herself on being a life-long learner.

ART LIZZA is a freelance writer with over 30 years' experience in scholarly publishing. Art resides in the relative wilderness of northwest New Jersey. He is adept at all facets of writing from conception, editing, copy editing, digital composition/manufacturing from printer files, print, CD & DVD production, and electronic delivery of publishing content. Art's motto: Uncompromising dedication to excellence, clarity, and accuracy.

SUE THOMPSON is the principal of Set Free Life Seminars, a speaking and training resource offering insights to help people become what they were meant to be, contributing confidently to life. She has a Master's degree in clinical psychology. Sue is a personality expert and etiquette trainer, and speaks to companies and organizations throughout the country.

LAWRENCE SCOTT has built his reputation with a solid technical background on delivering solutions to the commercial and industrial market place. A chemical engineer with over 25 years of experience, Lawrence has worked with many companies in Honolulu to address their particular air conditioning and energy related project needs. His firm, A/C Project Management, Inc., provides turnkey installations utilizing locally licensed contractors. Lawrence seeks to connect the Hawaiian islands' environmental needs with the realities of today's energy cost saving requirements.

SATORI SHAKOOR is a published writer, produced playwright, and a veteran of live performance. Satori received a 2007 NAACP Theatre Award for "Best Ensemble Cast" for her role as Ms. Enid in *Da Kink in My Hair*. She has recorded and toured as one of The Brides of Funkenstein and with George Clinton's Parliament/Funkadelic. Satori has worked with multiple Grammy award winners, including David Foster, the late Sly Stone, and Luther Vandross. She was an opening act for Joan Rivers, has appeared at The Improvisation, The Comedy Store and Yuk Yuk's. Theatre and film credits: *Harlem Duet, Boy Gets Girl, The Adventures of a Black Girl in Search of God, Menopause: The Musical!* and *The Hurricane*. Satori has written sketch comedy for Canadian television and her short story, "How I Took a Menopause" is published in an anthology entitled *Midlife Clarity: Epiphanies of Grown Up Girls*. For more info, visit: www.myspace.com/satorishakoor

ALFORD DAY is a fictional name. Although the story is true, at the time this book was published the author is litigating his case.

ALICIA M. NAILS is an Emmy-award winning television producer and journalist with more than twenty years' experience documenting and communicating the African American experience in both local and national media. She currently directs the Journalism Institute for Minorities at Wayne State University, in Detroit, Michigan. Alicia has written and produced at WTVS (PBS) and WJBK (Fox 2) in Detroit, WXIA (Atlanta), and for the formerly nationally syndicated *Essence* television program. She is currently a writer/editor at WWJ News Radio 950 in Detroit. Previously the National Marketing Director for United Methodist Communications in New York City, Alicia has extensive event organization skills, including special event production for the United Negro College Fund's Atlanta and Detroit offices, where she coordinated community and corporate leaders in fundraising events: the UNCF Parade of Stars Telethon, The Mayors' Scholarship Ball, and the *Ebony* Fashion Fair. An attorney, Alicia is licensed to practice in Michigan and Illinois.